Enjoy
Leicester
Libraries

Services and Public Libraries

CHANDOS
INFORMATION PROFESSIONAL SERIES

Series Editor: Ruth Rikowski
(email: Rikowskigr@aol.com)

Chandos' new series of books are aimed at the busy information professional. They have been specially commissioned to provide the reader with an authoritative view of current thinking. They are designed to provide easy-to-read and (most importantly) practical coverage of topics that are of interest to librarians and other information professionals. If you would like a full listing of current and forthcoming titles, please visit our web site **www.chandospublishing.com** or contact Hannah Grace-Williams on email info@chandospublishing.com or telephone number +44 (0) 1865 884447.

New authors: we are always pleased to receive ideas for new titles; if you would like to write a book for Chandos, please contact Dr Glyn Jones on email gjones@chandospublishing.com or telephone number +44 (0) 1865 884447.

Bulk orders: some organisations buy a number of copies of our books. If you are interested in doing this, we would be pleased to discuss a discount. Please contact Hannah Grace-Williams on email info@chandospublishing.com or telephone number +44 (0) 1865 884447.

Youth Services and Public Libraries

SUSAN E. HIGGINS

Chandos Publishing

Oxford · England

Chandos Publishing (Oxford) Limited
Chandos House
5 & 6 Steadys Lane
Stanton Harcourt
Oxford OX29 5RL
UK
Tel: +44 (0) 1865 884447 Fax: +44 (0) 1865 884448
Email: info@chandospublishing.com
www.chandospublishing.com

First published in Great Britain in 2007

ISBN:
978 1 84334 156 7 (paperback)
978 1 84334 167 3 (hardback)
1 84334 156 5 (paperback)
1 84334 167 0 (hardback)

© Susan E. Higgins, 2007

British Library Cataloguing-in-Publication Data.
A catalogue record for this book is available from the British Library.

The Publishers make no representation, express or implied, with regard to the accuracy of the information contained in this publication and cannot accept any legal responsibility or liability for any errors or omissions.

The material contained in this publication constitutes general guidelines only and does not represent to be advice on any particular matter. No reader or purchaser should act on the basis of material contained in this publication without first taking professional advice appropriate to their particular circumstances.

Typeset by Avocet Typeset, Chilton, Aylesbury, Bucks.
Printed in the UK and USA.

Contents

Preface

This book provides an overview of the principles of public library service to youth as they have evolved from their historical beginnings and interprets these principles in the light of modern practice. Quoting Virginia Matthews (2004), Michael Sullivan writes: 'Children's library services have a strong tradition of reaching out to the underserved and the underprivileged, and an association between children's services and social services still exists in the minds of both practitioners and the public' (Sullivan, 2005: 5). The association between children's services and social services can be seen as representative of a strong public service and humanitarian link. Today the manifestations of educational and economic policy and other societal underpinnings of library service to youth (such as libraries functioning as deterrents to crime) are well known. Such underpinnings take on new meaning, however, as quality-of-life issues proceed to the forefront of global consciousness and technology takes a front seat.

Youth Services and Public Libraries offers strategies to match the information needs and wants of children and young adults in public libraries and translates these into knowledge for providing relevant services. These services address the need for a highly educated workforce, a workforce which engages in lifelong learning and a workforce where inequalities are addressed and governments held accountable. The latest trends in service provision are covered within the context of the appropriate management, programming and marketing of services. Because the book is grounded in the principles of public library services to children and young adults everywhere, it links the practical application of library programming to the theoretical foundations of service and illustrates concepts with reference to the developmental needs of children and young adults. It describes how to implement library policies which recommend, design, direct, supervise and evaluate active youth services programs. Strategies to maximize access to services and sources are recommended as well as strategies to address public relations and marketing the library service to children and young adults.

This book is intended for library school students and practitioners and staff in public libraries. Some of the thematic topics discussed are the children's library as a social agency, issues and trends in the library service to young people, types of programs for different ages, the planning, execution and evaluation of programs, and the relationship between school and public libraries.

Introduction

Public libraries were developed in America, Europe and Australia in the mid-nineteenth century to promote and encourage the act of reading. Despite considerable changes in appearance as a result of the introduction at the end of the twentieth century of information technology and electronic access to information, the public library has been maintained with these foundational principles in mind. The public library as a place where reading is experienced as a social event is an identity which has held true for generations of people. And as Wayne Weigand has written:

> The scholarship on the social nature of reading and the concept of public space as a site for the construction of community suggest that the personal touch readers' advisors exercise intuitively makes them integral parts of these social dynamics. (Weigand, 2006: 11)

The personal touch that children's librarians bring to their communities sets the stage for lifelong reading. Because so many children visit the public library with their parents, children's librarians can generate the highest profile of service within the community. Parents acknowledge the role of the library and librarians in assisting the intellectual and prosocial behavior of their children, and through their familiarity with children and parents in their community, children's librarians can increase their effectiveness. This service concept of 'Youth as Persons' was put forward by

Adkins and Higgins (2006) as the most demonstrable feature in curriculum studies of youth services librarianship itself. It should be the guiding force of the reader's advisory work because consideration of children as individuals is related to the welcome they receive and is an ethical mode of service. Creating a nurturing environment addresses the social responsibility of children's librarianship in terms of knowledge of its professional, altruistic role. The deep-seated dynamics of social responsibility, justice, respect and love are the inner convictions that must be cultivated towards the humanization of human relations in children's libraries. In many respects youth librarians have the responsibility to make libraries (as well as schools) hospitable and inclusionary places for young people. Individuals are drawn to serve children and youth in public libraries through the advocacy or mission statement of their institutions and through the desire to interact with this client group in a positive and humanistic fashion. As Professor Adele Fasick notes, this is a subset of the basic mandate of service: 'We welcome and support all people in their enjoyment of reading and pursuit of lifelong learning' (Fasick, 1991). Such a welcome is inclusive in that it involves the building of a developmentally appropriate collection for youth, the importance of the reference interview with youth, excellent library programs and cooperation with schools in terms of providing supplementary resource materials and homework support.

Why do we serve children and young adults in public libraries? We serve them to assist in their personal development. We serve them because we are committed to their growth. We serve them because of our aesthetic appreciation of children's and young adult literature as well as theirs. In 'The future of the Earth' (1997), Tadahi Matsui wrote: 'The most powerful support and nucleus of power for children, I believe, is probably their experience in words and trust in words.' Experience and trust in words begin the educational journey. It is important to acknowledge that the public library is the only public institution which serves preschoolers. Parents who bring their preschoolers to the public library are aware that raising children to be highly individualistic, intellectually clever and self-motivated to the exclusion of others around them clearly has its limits. Personal development needs to include an awareness of the empathetic response. It has been said that children have much in common as they enter the twenty-first century. The differences in their ability to use and understand media are minimal compared to their differences in economic class and the ability to read. Research into the benefits of reading must be linked to the services available in public libraries for children and young adults. According to Adele Fasick:

> Public libraries were created to decrease social divisions and give children from working-class families, many of whom are also racial or ethnic minorities, a chance to compete at the same level with other children. This role as a force for social justice may be increasingly important in the early years of the twenty-first century as a counterbalance to conservative political agendas. (Fasick, 1998: xv)

Related to Fasick's statement is how the culture of community fostered in the public library benefits the life of the adult, child or young adult. This sense of community can give public library members identity, build commitment to the organization, build stability into the social system and make sense of the organization relative to the interests of the various participants (adapted from Sannwald, 2000).

The differences in economic class are indeed profound. Youth services librarians are partners in emergent literacy with daycare centers and partners with schools in the social enhancement and aesthetic appreciation of literature.

About the author

Susan E. Higgins received both her Bachelor of Arts degree in Creative Writing and her MLS from the University of Arizona in Tucson, AZ. After working as a children's librarian for Mesa Public Library in Mesa, AZ and Maricopa County Library in Phoenix, AZ she received a Department of Education Title II B Grant to enroll in the PhD program at Florida State University. Her dissertation was entitled *A Study of the Effectiveness of Public Library Service to Young Adults*. She currently teaches classes in children's literature, collection development and public librarianship at the University of Southern Mississippi School of Library and Information Science, Hattiesburg, MS. She has taught in Australia at Charles Sturt University, Wagga Wagga, NSW and in Singapore at Nanyang Technological University. She is an Adjunct Lecturer for Charles Sturt University School of Information Studies. Her research interests are education for library and information science, international children's literature and the aesthetic experience of reading in youth.

The author may be contacted via the publishers.

Part 1

Principles of Library Service

Historical beginnings: food for the young mind

Both elitism and paternalism were strong elements in the early public library movement, particularly with the poor and the young. It was the poor and the young families who made up the majority of immigrants at the turn of the twentieth century, and their successful assimilation into the American way of life was necessary as the basis of democracy and an informed electorate. Women involved in this cultural accommodation shared the common mission of bringing books of value to children.

The enjoyment and interpretation of literature for children emphasized nurturing the reading habit, which at its core was meant to create pride in belonging to America, reading, writing and speaking English, and becoming an American. In the manner of a father dealing benevolently and somewhat intrusively with his children, services for youth evolved as a practice of managing and governing individuals and groups through educational support. The development of the intellect became as important as the development of the body. The missionary zeal exhibited by children's librarians revolved around the concept of creating new citizens who in turn would support their community public libraries as adults. Such a citizen would read and access information critically and promote social justice. A government in which the supreme power is vested in the people and exercised directly by them deserved nothing less.

The concept of America as a meritocracy and libraries as places to acquire cultural knowledge of America is acknowledged as one of Andrew Carnegie's motivations to donate money from his steel factories to the establishment of public libraries at the turn of the twentieth century.

Carnegie wanted to give back to a nation which had made him a multi-millionaire and he believed that public libraries were a way that immigrants could become responsible citizens (Lorenzen, 2002). America continues to be a nation of minority populations and educational responsibilities are still engaged in assimilating children from different language backgrounds. Citing Bernhardt (1991), Mayra C. Daniel (2005) wrote: 'Because research suggests reading ability to be a stable and enduring second language modality, helping linguistic minority populations achieve literacy must be the top priority of our nation's schools.' That children and families achieve literacy is also an enduring priority of youth services in public libraries.

Public libraries in the United States

Kay Vandergrift (1996) and Virginia Walter (2001) traced the development of services to children in public libraries to the US Bureau of Education report entitled *Public Libraries in the United States*, which was commissioned in 1876, the same year the American Library Association (ALA) was founded. William I. Fletcher (1876) insisted that libraries should change their policies that limited access to children, and so the purposeful basis for children's services in public libraries became one of full access for children to library materials and services (Immroth, 1989). The task of accommodating children in public libraries was considered the 'social housekeeping' of the Progressive era, 1900–29. The connection between women coming to the forefront in the Progressive era was due to the lack of female suffrage. Anthony and Elizabeth Cady Stanton founded the National Woman Suffrage Association in 1869. It is important to remember that Child Labor Laws were not passed until the late 1800s and even today, according to recent global estimates by the International Labor Office, the number of working children aged 5 to 14 in developing countries is approximately 250 million. Of these, approximately 120 million work full-time in various jobs and often under hazardous conditions. In developing countries, a surplus of unskilled workers and low wages have combined to create conditions for children similar to the worst features of factories, mines and mills from the 1800s.

As women's organizations advocated to gain the right to vote, they also worked for broad-based economic and social reforms. By the beginning of the new century, women's clubs in towns and cities were working to promote suffrage, better schools, the regulation of child labor, women in unions and liquor prohibition. Not surprisingly, the essentially nurturing jobs affiliated with such social reform fell to women (Library of Congress). The call for social reform is historically affiliated with feminism and public service. According to Vandergrift, for the women who pioneered library service to children:

> As women of culture, their sense of self must have been that of those who, because of their educational, aesthetic, and cultural advances, felt a responsibility to improve the social situation and the taste of others by introducing them to the richness available in great literature. (Vandergrift, 1996: 685).

Dorothy Canfield Fisher spoke of the character of children's librarians:

> All over the United States (and increasingly in other democracies), they stand, these eager servers of young minds, these experts in intellectual and cultural

Children's room, Carnegie Library, Dorothy Gilliland, Children's Librarian (*c.*1960s)

(Reproduced courtesy of the Hemet Public Library Local History Collection.)

hygiene, bending earnestly over frowzy and well-kept young heads, valuing one no more than the others, trying to guess whether the gray matter inside the heads needs at this stage of development the rose of poetry, the spinach of history, the candy of fiction, or the bread of real study. (Fisher, 1929: 3)

The Dorothy Canfield Fisher Children's Book Award named after her is a unique award for new American children's books – the winner is chosen by the vote of child readers. Other outstanding women in children's services – Effie L. Power, Anne Carroll Moore, Lillian H. Smith, Mildred Bachelder, Bertha Mahoney Miller, Mary Wright Plummer, May Hill Arbuthnot, Augusta Baker, Margaret Edwards, Virginia Haviland and Charlotte Huck – shared complex institutional and interpersonal relationships in their quest to serve young minds. Public library concern for children, books and one another brought them together. As Lillian H. Smith wrote, 'The important point to remember is that children's reading, unlike that of adults, is conditioned by what is at hand' (1939: 125). These women helped to raise reading and literature to a higher level and allowed children not only access to books, but also to guidance and stimulation of their right to read. As Director of Work with Children at the Cleveland Public Library, Effie L. Power wrote:

> The purpose of a children's library is to provide children with a wide variety of good books supplemented by an inviting library environment and intelligent, sympathetic service and by these means to inspire and cultivate in them love of reading, discriminating taste in literature, and judgment and skill in the use of books as tools. (1928: 15)

Anne Lundin (1996) quoted Bertha Mahoney Miller, founder of the Horn Book. In 1936, Miller stated that the surge in children's book publishing could be attributed to 'the American heritage clamoring for expression, to the development of children's rooms in public libraries, and to the emergence of an outstanding group of women editors' (p. 200).

Reading in adolescence

Young adult service as a specialty grew naturally and distinctly out of children's services, which introduced pleasure reading for the purpose of enjoying language, absorbing thoughts and ideas, acquiring information and relaxing. Mary K. Chelton (1983) wrote that Mabel Williams began a separate service for young people in 1919 at the New York Public Library, and that much of Williams's career involved convincing adult departments to provide resources beyond textbooks for young adults and hire staff suited to work with young people.

Jean Piaget (1977) equated the beginning of adolescence with the beginning of formal operational thought. The adolescent's thoughts can be seen to correspond to formal, scientific, logical thinking. Although not all people attain the formal operations level, this era begins at approximately age 11. Programming and services for young adults are intended to appeal to ages 12–18. Personality development in adolescence precedes the adult role of acquiring skills and attitudes for occupations and is a social adaptation. Besides school peers, family and teachers who aid in this adaptation, books chosen by young adults themselves have the most to offer adolescents engaged in the process of personality development. According to Grams (1969), reading in adolescence is an emotional rather than an intellectual activity – reading is a social adaptation that is humanistic rather than technical in orientation.

The developmental assets of young adults require focus on improving reading for pleasure and interpersonal and cultural competence (Benson et al., 1999). Reading for recreation fulfils a strong developmental need of social interaction between peers. Choices involving education, health, careers, personal relationships and societal interactions are also being made and then remade, and then, of course, there is the variability of young adolescents – those between the ages of 12 and 15 demand a broad scope of collection provision, programming and activities. Young adults make heavy use of public libraries for schoolwork. In the 1960s, Lowell Martin found that the Enoch Pratt Free

Library in Baltimore tended to be used heavily by young adults who preferred the public library over the school library because it had more to offer in terms of resources (Martin, 1963). At that time both public and school libraries had an inadequate provision of student materials.

In 1901, Mary Wright Plummer, an 1888 graduate of Columbia Library School, accepted an appointment at the Pratt Institute Free Library. Public libraries themselves were considered the great accommodators of citizenship and deterrents to crime. The bookseller John Newbery was the first to publish exclusively for children in 1744. Newbery began publishing the research of the Brothers Grimm as a collection of folktales that are still children's favourites today. Miriam Ruth Gutman Braverman (1920–2002) was a socialist, activist librarian and longstanding member of the Progressive Librarians Guild, a founder of ALA's Social Responsibilities Round Table and a proponent of the social responsibilities perspective. Braverman was renowned for her spirit of activism and faith in the power of people's collective efforts toward social justice. In *Youth, Society, and the Public Library*, Braverman (1979) wrote that the schism between the capacity of the individual for self-realization and the materialistic realities of the industrial-technological system seems to plague each generation of children. Margaret Edwards (1969) wrote the classic text on young adult services, *The Fair Garden and the Swarm of Beasts*. She stated emphatically that a major failure of the urban public library was its insistence on curriculum-based services to young adults rather than concern for the individual in society. Today, the research of Keith Curry Lance and Becky Russell (2004) is frequently cited. Lance and Russell give empirical evidence as to the link between academic performance and well-resourced media centers and evidence of the impact of the school media librarian.

The view of the value of helping the young adult achieve as an independent, lifelong learner is widely acknowledged. Support for recreational reading as well as deep learning and critical thinking comes from dedicated librarians and well resourced libraries. The new technologies have created ethical dilemmas in the education of youth, just as they did during the Industrial Revolution with the practice of child labor. The Social Responsibilities Round Table of the ALA has as a purpose statement that members agree to promote social responsibility as a core value of librarianship. Such a core value of common good addresses these ethical dilemmas. Librarians have no control over the effect that an Internet site or a book will have on a particular reader at a given moment in time but they can build well stocked print collections for young adults who are ready to think critically and need encouragement. They can encourage decision-making among young adults. In his keynote address to the Canadian Library Association in 2004, ALA President Michael Gorman wrote, 'an illiterate with a computer is no better off than an illiterate with a book. Skill in reading and writing is as vital to the effective use of computers as it is to all other forms of communication' (2004: n.p.). Skill in reading has multidimensional application. Lee Shiflett placed the book in the context of other technological innovations when he wrote:

> The strength of the book remains in its ability to deliver a linear narrative and to develop an argument through the logical sequence of postulates, instances, and events. For this, the book will prevail and remain the preferred form of communication device. (2001: 48)

Shiflett writes that electronic forms celebrate the book. Even if, as forms of communication, electronic media are more effective, versatile and less expensive, changes in technology do not result in the complete replacement of one form by another. Technology itself is accumulative by nature. In 1984, Adele Fasick wrote: 'There are fundamental ways in which the uses of visual rather than printed materials, and computers rather than linear texts affect the way in which people find information and experience literature' (Fasick, 1984: 407). Twenty years later, we are still analysing how interactive computer portals invite participation and exploration in the information-seeking process and how information-seeking and cognition are linked. For children learning the language by being read to, and trying to speak the language and gauge the reaction to what they say, one can readily observe how this method mimics thinking itself and how the narrative structure grows in complexity with elements of story. Youth services librarians must decide which topics are best handled by print and continue to teach elementary school children how to use indices and tables of contents in informational books, but they must also determine the appropriateness of an electronic source when this access point is more beneficial for the project at hand.

Even though youth may prefer web collections, MySpace, blogs and interactive games to the book, young adults need the socialization and story provided by the library as place, not just for the popular print collections and Internet access to electronic books, although these too can be part of the social milieu. And even though young adults will often tell librarians that they use the library primarily for research on school-related projects and see little use of a special librarian to assist them, the special librarian indirectly assists in creating the 'information commons'. The developmental approach to serving children and teens in libraries is culturally sensitive – sensitive to the information and socialization needs of youth just as it was at the turn of

Two African-American children read books in the Freedom Library of the Palmers Crossing Community Center (*c.*1964). The books had been donated by many people all over the US

(Reproduced courtesy Herbert Randall Freedom Summer Collection, McCain Library and Archives, University of Southern Mississippi.)

the twentieth century with Braverman's treatise. How technology can meet the socialization needs of youth is a challenge for parents and libraries, as ethical dilemmas such as safety in cyberspace remain. The other side of the coin is that the potential for creativity and engagement with literature and authors is unsurpassed in the virtual world. The connectivity of professional online resources for librarians to serve and evaluate their service community is also unsurpassed.

Successful independence from parents and civic responsibility is often interpreted in its economic sense, as standing on one's own feet financially by holding down a job. It takes time to interpret independence as being able to contribute. In young adulthood, independence occurs incrementally and unevenly on a number of fronts. Step by step, young people achieve independence from their parents by establishing values and beliefs of their own, making their own choices and eventually by the physical separation of leaving home, either permanently or for extended periods. This growing independence goes hand in hand with the process of establishing separate identities and eventually new intimacies. The public library itself was once seen as an alternative to crime because of the perceived power of positive socialization and the acclimation to education it could provide for young people.

Mae Benne (1991) wrote that the children's librarian has responsibility for designing a program of service which is compatible with the mission of the library as well as the needs of the community. This concept of the children's library as a responsive, political and social agency justifies the funds for public libraries and the funds for children's librarians' salaries. Libraries are civic investments in the development of youth of all ages, and the power of reading to enrich the lives of children and young adults is foundational.

Providing appropriate programming would be considered essential to engaging the literacy skills of children even today, and continues to be a flagship of professional children's librarianship. Welcoming all members of the family to the library and its resources is a significant service aspect. Children's librarians have knowledge of the books in the collection, the popular websites for children to enjoy, the programming and activities available, an interest in popular culture and an understanding of the developmental stages of childhood and adolescent psychology. Programs are designed to be compatible with the key stages and cognitive models of child development and psychology.

Familiarity with the literature on childhood development falls within the purview of the children's librarian because this literature informs him or her of the social and human needs of children in the community. The development theories of Lev Vygotsky point to the need for a friendly intermediary to be supportive emotionally of children because they experience life in the affective domain – this was named 'the zone of proximal development' (Vygotsky, 1987).

Personal intervention on the part of librarians is indicative of promoting individualized learning for youth. Carol Kuhlthau and Ross Todd (2004) report:

> The personal touch of the professional school librarian matters a great deal to the students. Personal engagement with students to initiate and enable learning and achievement is a critical component of an effective school library. School librarians who have a clearly defined role as an information-learning specialist and perform in this way play a vital role in enabling students to learn through information.

Krashen (1993) wrote that information and knowledge can be conceptualized as types of developmental needs and that the implications for library service to children can be deduced from these needs. Children's library services and family literacy are important areas for research in children's literature and such areas address the power of narrative. Narrative is powerful because it takes place within the social organization. Hearne refers to the field of children's publishing as a 'professional matriarchy of children's books': 'The values, codes, and consolidations of the profession are passed on in stories that serve the function of, and bear many resemblances to, family narrative' (Hearne, 1996: 755)

Promotion of storytelling and reading are important, but research into learning, parenting, leadership and training and support for community agencies is also needed by the youth services librarians of tomorrow. Since children's librarians address the needs of a population of great diversity in age, cultural background, ethnicity and primary language, they need to be willing to assume a leadership role in the specialization's professional community. The traditional core skills of librarianship can offer reading intervention for children and large benefits for society can be reaped. Bob Usherwood (2003) quoted the *Framework for the Future* report (Benson et al., 1999), which stated that 'the modern mission of libraries should be based on four main factors. These are identified as evolution, public value, distinctiveness, and local interpretations of national programmes' (p. 305). Similarly, Gobinda Chowdhury sees the public library as an ideal location to disseminate local knowledge in physical and electronic formats. Focusing on the public library as a community knowledge hub will bring this knowledge to the niche market it serves. Beyond the online catalog, the public library web page can function as a portal designed to meet the needs of users. Chowdhury writes: 'We see the possibility of each public library using a standard system (yet to be developed) to enable each one to act as a local knowledge hub but also to allow its resources to be accessible by other local knowledge hubs or by any user on the internet' (Chowdhury et al., 2006: 456). This gives a sense of place to the youth of the community as well as all other public library users. McCook states: 'The public library provides a sense of place that can transcend new development, big-box stores, and malls, to help a community retain its distinct character' (2004: 294). Such transcendence is based on the non-commercial aspect and sense of belonging to the local community which the public library makes possible.

The introduction of computers into children's services departments in North America has brought computers to the forefront of literacy efforts. However, computer services to children imply the ability to interpret what is on the screen and the ability to read and spell correctly in order for 'computer meaning' to emerge from the information topics sought. Younger children prefer to go directly to the shelves or ask a friend or parent for help and the richness of response to print collections is multidimensional in creating readers. For school-age children, Walter (2003) writes, 'public libraries, particularly those offering after-school homework assistance programmes, need to consider augmenting the training that young students get in school.' The children's librarian role emerges perhaps more strongly today as an intermediary between the children, their siblings, parents or caregivers and the resources of the library – a traditional role in the digital age. Children's librarians also provide the context for sharing information. Parents and caregivers exchange day-to-day information relevant to their activities in the social context of the public library. A collection of parenting materials within the youth services collection is entirely appropriate to support such needs.

At the other end of the principles spectrum, what brings most young adults into the public library is related to school assignments. The Voice of Youth Advocates (VOYA) bases its policy on these three principles:

- *Specialized YA library services.* Young adults aged 12–18 deserve their own targeted library services, collections and attention to the same extent as populations of other ages.
- *Intellectual freedom and equal access.* Young adults have rights to free and equal access to information in print, non-print and electronic resources, without infringement of their intellectual freedom due to age or other restrictions.
- *Youth advocacy and youth participation.* Youth-serving professionals must advocate for the above rights and services for youth within their libraries, schools, and communities, while providing opportunities for youth to practise decision-making and responsibility in running their own projects.

Reading and information-seeking

The relationship of reading and information-seeking in services to youth is that they are tied to lifelong literacy through the concept of personal information-seeking. Personal information-seeking is the most significant kind of information-seeking process. Children and young adults are most likely to be engaged in personal information-seeking in libraries, and even if the query is imposed by someone else, as in a school assignment, the information-seeking itself remains personal and within the affective domain.

Interactive electronic books of popular children's selections offer interactivity and motion; however, the portability and privacy of the printed book is a key factor in its popularity, at least with girls. The traditional book relates to the personal world of the individual in a way that computers do not. Gender differences do exist, many educators believe technology itself is gendered, and boys reading in the non-fiction area of machines and computers may prefer to read about such topics online and to work alone. The computing culture has not incorporated girls to the extent which inclusion implies. Collaborative work is a key aspect of gender equality, and learning needs to become a social not an individual event (Higgins, 2000/1). Socially responsible initiatives in classrooms and appropriate programming in public libraries can convince girls that ability in science and mathematics is natural and appropriate. Educators feel a growing commitment to involve girls and their families in female education as part of the push for gender equity because families have a great stake in their children's education.

As formats evolve, the experience of being in the library should be a comfortable and positive one primarily because, in the virtual world, children can talk and play with friends, play sports, watch films, create illustrated stories with software, etc. Cell phones and laptops are capable of text messaging, sending e-mail, browsing the Internet and listening to MP3s, but in the physical public library, the book is an irreplaceable foundation of literacy.

Knowledge of reading preferences brings to the forefront the communication dimension of work, with youth as a significant, qualitative component of practice. Children's librarians, the majority of whom were women, were charged to question the selection of sources in terms of a balanced appeal to both genders. The opportunity to arouse children's interest in reading and learning, information and libraries, is still seen as short-lived. Exploiting this interest while children are still in full-time education is the job of youth services librarians.

Children's literature through social history

Generally speaking, trends in reading and literature follow the social standing of the child in society. At one time, children were considered miniature adults and were offered no protection. Child labor laws did not come into effect until 1900, so many children worked and died under horrific conditions in coal mines in the USA. In fact, it is said that Carnegie Libraries were built on the backbone of steel workers, that the millions Andrew Carnegie gave to establish American public libraries served to assuage his guilt over children dying in the mines – this was the dark side of his philanthropy. At one time, there were no schools to protect children from exploitation, and their parents needed their earnings to support the family. Referring to the last two decades of the nineteenth century, Walter writes that John Dewey's ideas about education, G. Stanley Hall's theories of child psychology and the establishment of the Child Study Association were particularly influential in bringing awareness to the plight of children and their social, physical, emotional and educational needs (2001: 2).

Aesop's fables (dating from at least the third or fourth century BC) marked the beginning of literature for children – children enjoyed reading the fables, even though they were written for an adult audience. From the Roman Empire to early Christianity up to the 1300s tales were told as a means of instruction but actually blended history with myth, fable and religion. Bestiaries (descriptions of animals with pictures) and courtesy books of the fourteenth century were didactic and solemn, intended to teach children proper behavior, and were particularly written for the sons of nobility as a means to inculcate etiquette. Hornbooks,[1] chapbooks and ABCs made their appearance in the late 1500s, and primers and readers date from the sixteenth century. Primers were alphabets and lists of vowels, consonants and syllables incorporated with religious content. Because adults viewed the young as having Original Sin, the New Testament was produced in rhymed couplets and intended for memorization. Divine emblems featured pictures chosen for their symbolic meaning and were combined with text to present brief moral or religious lessons. As many children did not survive the first five years of life, preparing them for the afterlife was seen as an obligation of parenthood.

By this time, entertaining the young had become an accepted technique in their moral education, and proverbs, maxims, adages and old wives' tales have always played an important part. For example, *Proverbs Exemplified* was written by John Trusler in 1790, and in 1807 Benjamin Franklin produced *Maxims and Morals*. In the eighteenth century, collections of proverbs or popular sayings also appeared, such as 'Birds of a feather flock together', 'A friend in need is a friend indeed' and 'Rome wasn't built in a day.' Proverbs are intuitively pleasing because they have so many applications to everyday life.

Present context of establishing a culture of literacy and lifelong learning

The present context of the establishment of a culture of literacy and lifelong learning is no different from the past – just more inclusive of children and their families. The key to living in a rapidly changing world lies in the mastery of technology – and lifelong learning encompasses such technology. Public librarians embrace both print and technology as essentially complementary aspects of resource provision. Establishing a social context of learning goes beyond the development of an aesthetic response and knowledge of what technology has to offer. Susanne Krueger and Rita Schmitt (1999) have said 'books are often much harder for children to interpret than audio-visual or electronic media.' Computers and technology are unlikely to replace books and reading in the education of young children because print provides the basic intellectual context for processing information and this intellectual context is narrative (Quek and Higgins, 2003). Technology supports the informal view of learning through non-competitive small-group discussion rather than the traditional view which involves a large class and exam-based drilling which ends when school ends. Today's youth are learning how to learn, and embrace the type of learning that engages understanding of oneself, other people and the world, in other words the social context of learning. Knowledge of the Digital Divide and the great disparity of economic wealth in the world is an example of the development of a worldview for teenagers.

The future of library services to children rests on the shoulders of parents who pay for such services with their taxes, and most importantly of those who visit the libraries with their children as they are more likely to know the purpose of a public library. Parenting itself is a major issue for society. Many notable women library leaders acknowledge the contribution of Kay Vandergrift to the profession of youth services librarianship. Vandergrift advocates feminist philosophy as foundational to children's literature classes because the state of the world's children is inexorably linked with the status of those most frequently involved with them – their families. Feminism is also related to the ethic of care. Vandergrift believes that in many library and information science departments, the priorities tend more towards 'science' than 'literature' or 'library'. The preoccupation of the profession with current technology and practice has further obscured attention to history.

Literacy and lifelong learning can also be related to developmental milestones in children. Catherine Blanshard summarized these milestones in *Managing Library Services for Children and Young People* (1998). From birth to age 2, the child experiences the world in a perceptual, action-oriented, mostly non-verbal way. Information is gained from them through their actions and behaviours. From age 2 to age 5 at the preschool level, the advent of language and symbolic action allows the young child to share meaning with others. At this age the child has a significant capacity for understanding and responding to adults if the subject is immediately related to the child's experiences. From 6 to 12, the child begins to think about what she or he says and reasons more logically. There is a growing adult-like ability to communicate and respond. The developmental phases generally described here can be incorporated with knowledge of the basic needs of childhood: the need to love and be loved, the need to belong, the need to achieve, the need for security – material, emotional, spiritual – and, finally, the need to know. Regardless of where the child might be developmentally, the basic needs of childhood prevail and how and why books speak to children revolve around such needs. Anthropomorphism is popular because children have empathy for the animals who speak, act and dress as human beings.

There is a further connection between lifelong literacy and the issue of censorship in that both concepts involve intellectual freedom and the right to read. Librarians need keep in mind that selection is a positive task meant to serve users and support programs. When complaints from parents or guardians regarding book selections occur, it is important for children's librarians to understand that the parents are most often acting on behalf of their children whom they wish to protect. Benne writes:

> The desire to protect children is not one that most of us would like to see eliminated from our society. The complainant's concern is worthy of respect, especially if it is apparent that this is a person who takes seriously her or his parental responsibilities. The children's librarian must recognize a parent's right to guide a child but not the right to impose standards on the community's children without following a procedure required by official policy. (Berne, 1991: 129)

Letting parents or guardians know that forms are available to make an official request for reconsideration often helps them to recognize that their complaint will be taken seriously. Often parents would just like to register their complaint verbally, and a diplomatic librarian will listen without becoming defensive. Complaints from parents can be seen as a way to market and promote the library because acknowledging these complaints can lead to a relationship in which the parents are encouraged to continuously evaluate what their children are reading or viewing. Professional librarians value feedback from their clientele.

Children and young people will eventually manage services for today's generation of adults. Educational policies in libraries, available via the mission statement and collection development policies, reflect this. The development of a literate middle-class public was critical for the continuance of the public library system in 1900, and such a principle remains foundational today. Even those who live in the community and do not use the public library view the public

An adolescent boy finds reading to be an interesting activity

(Photo by Branislav Ostojic. Courtesy Shutterstock 2007.)

library as a social good. The presence of a good public library in a town, city or county spurs economic growth.

Continuing inequalities in development throughout the world underscore the need for the children of today to enter the world of science and technology tomorrow. The library can be the first step in terms of cultural adaptation and 'the modernization of mentalities' (Delors, 1996: 13). Delors also writes:

> In confronting the many challenges that the future holds in store, humankind sees in education an indispensable asset in its attempt to attain the ideals of peace, freedom and social justice. As it concludes its work, the Commission affirms its belief that education has a fundamental role to play in personal and social development. The Commission does not see education as a miracle cure or a magic formula opening the door to a world in which all ideals will be attained, but as one of the principal means available to foster a deeper and more harmonious form of human development and thereby to reduce poverty, exclusion, ignorance, oppression and war. (Delors, 1996: 11)

Constant growth in public libraries serving families presupposes the place of the library in the economic policy of the community.

Children's rights today

The first Children's Rights Convention was convened by the United Nations in November of 1989. Some 190 countries have now signed the Convention which is based on the principle that every child and young person, regardless of their sex, race, economic circumstances or disability, has equal rights that should be respected. The Convention also recognizes that children are more vulnerable to mistreatment and abuse and need special care and protection. More than 40 articles in the Convention address children's rights, but six main principles are pre-eminent:

1. Every child, regardless of race, colour, sex, language, religion or disability, should be protected from all kinds of discrimination (Article 2).

2. Everyone dealing with children is obligated to consider the children's best interests in the matter before them and to provide the children with the care and protection they need (Article 3).

3. Every child has the right to life, survival and development (Article 6).

4. Every child capable of forming an opinion shall be given the opportunity to express that opinion and have it taken into account (Article 12).

5. Every child has the basic right to a family (Article 17).

6. Children and parents have mutual rights and responsibilities within the family environment which are paramount in a child's upbringing (Articles 18–20).

Groups of underclass exist in every country. Six groups of children are at risk of severe disadvantage from social and/or economic hardship:

- children of single parents;
- children of the long-term unemployed;
- many minority children;
- all homeless children;
- wards of the state;

- young people affected by mental illness.

Advertising can have a negative affect on children as it inculcates attitudes of materialism and acquisitiveness and fosters anti-social attitudes; it also encourages unhealthy dietary habits. Television often portrays a white, Anglo-Saxon, male-dominated, middle-class world whereas the people who make up the population of the United States are diverse in race, religion, and national origin. Heather Neff wrote that multiculturalism is a concept that has formed the very fabric of the American nation from the beginning:

> American insistence on the importance of plurality – the beauty, richness, and ultimate democracy that are obtained by the harmonization of many disparate voices – lies a true sense of the tensions which drive this nation to retain its character, its color, its unity. (Neff, 1996: 50)

As libraries strive to be centres of creativity and innovation in society, cultural diversity provides the richness where new ideas can be generated. Diversity in libraries can be demonstrated by collection holdings of multicultural fiction and non-fiction and by the staff and administrators. Neff notes that Jim Henson Productions and a plethora of Children's Television Workshop projects present culturally diverse work in their films. However, black, Latino, Native American or Asian characters need to be portrayed more frequently in heroic roles. Native folktales tend to fill a void for children who are seeking identity and solace in children like themselves – children portrayed in a positive light. In the article 'Exploring prejudice in young adult literature through drama and role play', Barbara Bontempo wrote: 'The adolescent years are timely years for dealing with issues of discrimination, prejudice, and cultural differences since adolescents often perceive themselves as a "culture" apart from the mainstream.' The potential for multicultural literature to communicate the complexity of human emotion and experience is profound.

Youth advocacy

Youth advocacy (YA) is just as much a requirement of tomorrow as science and technology, knowledge of self and the environment, and the development of skills which enable people to live harmoniously. For youth services librarians, youth advocacy is also about choice. The capacity of youth to make decisions in their own lives, even if those decisions are incorrect, is seen as a road to healthy identity. If youth can obtain what they want and make critical choices, they will find themselves at a rich intersection of print, electronic media and the affective learning process. The social adaptation of decision-making can be addressed through the development of social competencies and facilitated through the use of technology. Committed youth services librarians champion the individual and are aware of age-appropriate and age-controversial literature. Computers cannot replicate human perceptual and conceptual capabilities, so the use of technology in libraries must be based on how well the children are served and not just on their ability to help themselves. Advocacy is based in calls for reform – just as it was with the suffragettes and in the factories of the Industrial Revolution. Today, perhaps the focus is on how the child can not only develop well, but thrive in a global environment of social justice. Key attributes of participation in civil society are the reasoning skills for making informed judgements, moral traits and practical experience in community organizations. Opportunities for practical experience in community organizations such as libraries assist young adults to work cooperatively.

In a report published by the UK's Department of Culture, Media and Sport in 2003, public libraries were charged to 'provide socially inclusive services' (Usherwood, 2003). The report identified evolution, public value, distinctiveness and local interpretations of national programs as emerging roles grounded in the traditional. Libraries were encouraged to maintain traditional core services and 'focus on areas where public intervention would deliver large benefits for society' (Usherwood, 2003). In the public library, advocacy for youth is meaningful and inclusive because the large benefits for society are immeasurable. Through promotion of reading and access to digital services, librarians advocate freedom of choice and thought, responsibility and engagement. Nowhere is the potential for such benefits more powerful than with youth clientele.

The library is a social agency for children and young adults. Youth services librarians are knowledgeable of issues and trends in library service to young people, and this includes knowledge of the community's schools. The relationship between school and public libraries is that both institutions are funded by taxpayers' money and the clientele is shared. Youth services librarians adhere to standards and practices such as a collection development policy and standards advocated by their national associations. They plan, carry out and evaluate programs in terms of the ability of the program to meet the goal of literacy. Library systems which employ YA librarians enjoy more participation by young adults in the community. If the employment of a specialist is not possible, service amenities such as increased emphasis on the collection of material of popular appeal, the provision of booklists on YA reading, and the provision of local information and referral pamphlets for crisis intervention are appropriate.

Children need help in choosing books and other materials and help in learning how they can be used – the children's librarian is focused on facilitating this learning environment. The preparation of recommended reading lists based on age level/reading level serve as handy tools for parents. Such bibliographic lists can be annotated. These lists, as well as being reference tools, serve the function of locating books which address specific problems – such as sibling rivalry, a new baby in the family, or learning table manners. Special files such as those with handouts for science projects are very popular.

The appeal of children's literature is focused on the values it holds for children, and reading focused on pleasure and information is the vehicle of understanding. Literacy is a multidimensional concept and, according to Adele Fasick (1984), the development of informational literacies in children undergird the management of children's library services in children's departments. This includes the management of personnel, perspectives on client groups, the planning of services, the evaluation of services, and writing and publicizing policies. Books appeal to the young because within their stories are the resources to help a child become aware of the beauty of words, to develop values to live by, to recognize that she or he is not alone in the world, and to identify an idea or cause which might guide him or her throughout life. Ultimately, talking about books with children aids their socialisation into society because such discussions hone their ability to make informed decisions about their lives and the lives of those around them. Librarians are advocates of literacy, and the practices of librarianship are the tools of such advocacy: providing resources, implementing programs, telling a story and connecting with the public all create communities of practice.

Youth advocacy begins with the personality characteristics which are associated with children's librarianship in terms of the professional relationship with the youth user. According to Benne (1991) these was as follows:

- The librarian does not need to be in control or stand as an acknowledged authority figure.
- The librarian is willing to perform before a less critical audience.
- The librarian is willing to set standards for children as exacting as those for adult service.
- The librarian is flexible in implementing policies.
- The librarian has respect for the dignity of the individual, the grace to learn from children, and the ability to laugh or sympathize with children as they learn to understand their world and the resources the library holds.

Advocacy has meaning on an organizational level as well. Youth services librarians can initiate community partnerships and collaborative ventures with schools, daycares, homeless shelters and charitable organizations in the area. They can press home the message of the importance of youth services to the director of the library using statistical analysis of attendance and circulation figures. They can codify how they assist students in using the Internet and clarify the library's role in the implementation of technology.

In conclusion, advocates for youth include librarians, trustees, Friends of the Library, library customers, and community and institutional leaders. Advocacy is thus an expression of commitment to engage in the democratic process.

Most important, [it includes] people of all ages and all walks of life who view the public library as an essential part of their community. Being an advocate means communication, as an individual or group, with decision makers and others in support of or opposition to specific issues. (Resource Guide for Directors, p. 5.5.1)

Advocacy is thus an expression of commitment to engage in the democratic process.

Youth services librarians as peacekeepers

Adele Fasick (1998) states that traditional youth services in public libraries exist in an entirely different milieu than in the past. Social trends reflecting change in family makeup require more accommodation on the part of the librarian; however, the need for youth librarians to be advocates for the child and teenager and to respect their privacy, and the need for the child or young adult to be socialized into reading and into the community at large, will not change. The communication dimension is significant in work with children and young adults as it is based on respect for the individual as a person. Such a character dimension in children's librarianship is necessary in order that information can be used to the advantage of human relations. Children's librarians accept the inculcation of a public service attitude as an ethical and professional stance of librarianship as a whole. Ismail Abdullahi quotes Natalia Tyulina, former Director of the Dag Hammerskjold Library

We live in a time when significant efforts are made by different countries, nations, and peoples toward better understanding of each other, the knowledge that mutual understanding is the most important condition for maintaining peace in the world. As technology acts as a cultural eraser, librarianship serves an increasingly important role, bringing together the records of the best achievement of humanity and the individual human being, thus helping to establish better understanding among people. In this respect our profession may be considered one of the 'peace-keeping tools. (*http:// darkwing.uroregon.edu/~felsing/ala/abdullahi.html*)

In 1930, Effie L. Power wrote that the library is a place for children to read for pleasure, that the vocation of children's librarianship 'seeks to make books vital factors in a child's life, and through service and books to prepare children for adult life' (Power, 1930: 296). After 75 years, her common-sense theory remains descriptive not only of the child's experience in the library and the purpose of the library as a vital place in family life, but the purpose of children's librarianship as facilitating and accommodating the natural curiosity of children throughout the world.

Literacy itself is a major global problem as acknowledged by the UN's establishment of the Literacy Decade 2003–2012:

> While societies enter into the information and knowledge society, and modern technologies develop and spread at rapid speed, 860 million adults are illiterate, over 100 million children have no access to school, and countless children, youth and adults who attend school or other education programmes fall short of the required level to be considered literate in today's complex world. (UNESCO, Bangkok)

An understanding of the international aspect of librarianship in work with youth in libraries has the potential to alleviate aspects of poverty associated with illiteracy. Libraries and literacy are associated with world peace. After the Second World World, the Jella Lepman Children's Library in Munich was established on the foundation of world peace for children. Lepman saw this as an opportunity for a new world emerging after the Nazi terror. Opened in 1949, it is an internationally recognized center for children's and youth literature of the world. The International Youth Library's heart is the collection of nearly 540,000 books, with 500,000 volumes of children's and youth books in more than 130 languages and nearly 30,000 titles of secondary literature. A thousand publishers from around the world send sample copies of their latest titles to the library each year. Approximately 9,000 books are cataloged annually (International Youth Library website). Moreover, the International Children's Digital Library (*http://www.icdlbooks.org/*) states as its purpose the idea of inspiring children to be part of the global community, by creating 'children who understand the value of tolerance and respect for diverse cultures, languages and ideas – by making the best in children's literature available online.'

Note

1. A child's primer, made of parchment, mounted on a board with a handle, protected by a transparent plate made of horn. (See: *http://www.trussel.com/books/glossary.htm* – accessed 11 January 2007.)

Part 2

Practices

Management of libraries for youth

Although the youth services librarian is faced with spending public money wisely in the face of technological change, how youth services librarians practise the art and science of the discipline is based on the service role taken in the interpretation of the child's or young adult's intellect. Reading in childhood enlarges one's empathy for oneself and the human condition. In adolescence, reading is also primarily an emotional experience. Adolescents need to interact with peers and acquire a sense of belonging. They need to discuss conflicting values and formulate their own value systems along with acquiring their own identity in relationships and with other people and ideas. Activities such as listening to music, watching television, reading popular magazines and books, and viewing movies, all contribute to peer interaction. Resources which support curriculum assignments for children and young adults are well used in public libraries. Students have a demanding curriculum and often need the library as a quiet place in which to study and complete homework. The nearly 60 million children born after 1979 will be the first to grow up in a world saturated with networks of information, digital devices and perpetual connectivity.

The rare birds: youth services librarians

The duties of children's librarians can be divided into administrative tasks, collection development tasks, programming and services. Administrative tasks include hiring, training and evaluating staff, liaison with library

Young adults using the adult collection (*c.*1960s)

(Reproduced courtesy of the Hemet Public Library Local History Collection.)

administration, service on library committees, settings goals and objectives, setting programming policies, giving input on facilities design, selecting decorations for the department, planning renovations, and giving inputs on the computer system. Collection development tasks include setting collection policies, the selection of materials, developing circulation policy, developing weeding and shelving policy, and handling complaints. Programming tasks cover setting policy for target groups, contacting schools for summer reading advertisements, designing publicity for programs, planning programs, and training staff to conduct programs. Services provided to children include the reference service, reading guidance, registration, planning and conducting user education, and assisting children with computer use. Youth services librarians keep in mind the following research questions as they serve their clientele:

- What characteristics differentiate children and young adults who use the library and those who do not?
- Are there changes in policy, services or collections which the library could make which would improve service to library users?
- Are there changes the library could make which might encourage non-users to make use of the library?

(Adapted from Fasick and England, 1977)

In the midst of such change, youth services librarians remain positive.

Information behavior

Feinberg et al. wrote:

> The vision of facilitated learning by children, families, and the community is based on the idea that all children can learn and are entitled to equitable access to cognitively enriching, socio-emotionally satisfying, and developmentally appropriate resources and learning opportunities. (1998: xiv)

It is important to view the information behaviour of children through the lens of the family. Andrew Shenton wrote that for children, the use of other people was the most frequently employed method of seeking information, and that the roles of particular individuals, such as parents, friends or teachers, often varied according to the child's information need.

Regardless of the type of need and their age, there were youngsters who tended to go to certain people for whom they had a high regard. Indeed, other people, more than any other form of source appear to transcend particular need types. (Shenton, 2003: 228)

Shenton recommended that issues associated with the use of other people should be dealt with in a similar way to those pertaining to books and electronic sources when dealing with the information needs and behaviors of children.

The report of the Young Adult Library Services Association, *Young Adults Deserve the Best: Competencies for Librarians Serving Young Adults* (2003), outlined seven areas of competency needed by librarians working with young adults in any type of information agency. These areas were leadership and professionalism, knowledge of the client group, communication, administration, knowledge of materials, access to information and services.

Denise E. Agosto and Sandra Hughes-Hassell (2006) constructed a model of the everyday life information needs of urban teenagers using written surveys, audio journals, activity logs, photographs and semi-structured group interviews in data collection. They coded the data into a theoretical model including seven areas of urban teen development: the social self, the emotional self, the reflective self, the physical self, the creative self, the cognitive self, and the sexual self. They concluded that teenagers seek everyday life information to facilitate their maturation process in these areas. Clearly teenagers move toward integration of identity in their information-seeking behaviours.

How libraries are managed is a function of developing these unique selling points of the purpose of literacy in the lives of children and teens. The mission statement of the public library acknowledges youth as important users in the community. Actions in the youth services department, from the management of people to collection management to the management of programming, revolve around the mission statement and consideration of how to support literacy development in the child. A parent's collection of books, videos, audio books, periodicals, electronic resources and pamphlets which focus on the provision of information on child development, reading and literature, activities for young children, health and nutrition, music and art education, child rearing and children with special needs help parents to better understand how to carry out their parenting role effectively. In their book entitled *Learning Environments for Young Children: Rethinking Library Spaces and Services*, Feinberg et al. wrote:

> Children's librarians need to be familiar with the entire range of adult services and seek opportunities to inform parents as potential users. Adults who may first enter the library to entertain their child or to enlarge their social group begin to expand their own education horizons. Information for adults within the secure early childhood setting may woo a reluctant adult into investigating additional library resources directed primarily to adult interest and needs. This sets in motion a cycle of continuous learning for all family members. (1998: 57)

Developing the library community's response to user needs is a participatory process through which librarians identify community needs and organize themselves to take the actions necessary to improve the quality of life for their constituents. In *Ladders to Literacy*, Notari-Syverson et al. (1998) wrote: 'The most important academic task that children accomplish in the elementary school years is the development of formal literacy.' Shenton and Dixon (2004b) noted that the home library was an important tool in the attainment of formal literacy because of its ready accessibility.

Interpretation of management principles for this particular audience also requires adaptation. Library policies which recommend, design, direct, supervise, and evaluate active youth services programs are at the core of good management. The collection development policy itself is a document of communication and addresses the needs of the community served. The needs of the special community of children are often addressed in the collection development policies of children's departments everywhere. Children's intellectual development and their personal and aesthetic response to literature can be seen as the heartbeat of children's librarianship in public libraries. The operational concept is the reference interview with children (which often occurs with their parents). The librarian can repeat the child's question to the child, ask for clarification from the parent or guardian, and also observe how the question may be related to the child's developmental stage.

Children's author Mem Fox (1992) used the phrase 'learning through delight': 'When books are read for their intended purposes of entertaining and informing, and when that entertainment and information bond readers and listeners in mutual delight, learning to read becomes an almost natural activity and an enormous pleasure' (Fox, 1992: 3).

Services to youth with special needs

Investing in Children: The Future of Library Services for Children and Young People was published in 1995 by the Library and Information Services Council (England) and quoted by John Vincent (2005: 2): '... children and young people have been taken to include those of minority ethnic origins, those with disabilities, and others whose needs may be regarded as being in some way special.' Vincent determined that children with special needs may indeed be 'shut out, fully or partially, from any of the political, social, cultural or economic systems which determine the social integration of a person in society'. Technological advances in education have been a boon for special needs children as have general developments in online learning environments. Youth with special needs can be accommodated very well in the physical and virtual public library; however, the librarian's attitude toward and experience with children with disabilities may affect program delivery and the librarian may have to adjust expectations for participation, for example. Taking part in library programs can prepare the child for the demands of the general school setting. Family members play a key role in providing information about the child's abilities and interests to the librarian. By identifying specific ways for parents to be involved in the story time process with their children, such as participating with them when the story time takes place, the librarian communicates the message that the library is a place of social inclusion.

According to the National Early Childhood Technical Assistance Center, the US federal government has an ongoing obligation to support activities that contribute to positive results for children with disabilities, enabling those children to lead productive and independent adult lives.

The Americans with Disabilities Act 1990 states that public accommodations must make reasonable modifications in policies, practices, and procedures in order to accommodate individuals with disabilities. However, a modification is not required if it would fundamentally alter the goods or services of a childcare setting. Architectural barriers must be removed if 'readily achievable.' The term 'readily achievable' means easily accomplishable and able to be carried out without much difficulty or expense (see National Network for Child Care). Bibliographies of disability resources for families and librarians are available from statewide and regional resource centers, along with print materials and suggestions for librarians working with patrons with certain disabilities. The Library of Congress National Library Service for the Blind and Physically Handicapped hosts an online Reference Section of materials and pamphlets for children's librarians, such as *Focus on Children: Story Hour at the Public Library: Ideas for Including Visually Impaired Preschoolers*. Provision of ample space for a child who uses a wheelchair to navigate successfully between shelves, resources such as books on tape, listening center equipment, and computer disks featuring various skill levels all promote library usage. Computer programs which address the needs of ESL (English as a Second Language) students are also available. Story time for special needs children does not require an extensive or different collection as they enjoy the same puppets and stories which appeal to both children and parents. Funding for the Captioned Media Program (CMP) is provided by the United States Department of Education and hosted by the National Association of the Deaf in Spartanburg, South Carolina. Media titles are available via Internet streaming, which allows viewers to read captioned media at their convenience. CMP also allows previewing in DVD or VHS format for preselection before borrowing. Family sign language and informational videos are also available. CMP supports the US Department of Education Strategic Plan for 2002–2007 and ensures that all deaf and hard of hearing students have the opportunity to achieve standards of academic excellence, advocates for accessible media, establishes and maintains the quality of captioning, involves its constituents in the selection, evaluation, production, and distribution of its products, and explores and adapts new media and technologies which assist people in using information. Children who have no vision, those partially sighted and those visually impaired may receive free library service at home if they are already using materials from the state library headquarters. The at-home library service can help the child participate in their public library's summer reading program and provide back-up reading required for school assignment. Parents may register their child online. The selection of appropriate stock or information about the provision of resources for special audiences is considered a method of social inclusion. The National Library Service (NLS) Reference Bibliographies offer a Kid Zone website. The National Dissemination Center for Children with Disabilities (NICHCY) addresses disabilities in infants, toddlers, children and youth, serving as a central source of information for IDEA (the Individuals with Disabilities Education Act) 2004 and the No Child Left Behind Act 2002 (as it relates to children with disabilities). Research-based information on effective educational practices is freely available.

Unattended children in the public library

Julie Arrighetti (2001) writes that unattended children in the public library pose a continuing challenge for librarians. Parents may be struggling to provide childcare arrangements and assume the public library is a safe place for their children. Many libraries have found that offering programs for unattended children is an excellent way to strengthen the relationship between the library and its community and will foster a new generation of library users. Not only is childhood use of the public library the best predictor of adult use, support for services for children is a primary reason why many adults support the contemporary public library today. Nevertheless, librarians note complaints from adult patrons about noise, damage and limited seating available when school is out for the day and children are within walking distance of the library. Due to security and safety concerns, many libraries have begun enforcing a minimum age for unattended children. Generally speaking, these state that every child under 11 must be accompanied by an adult over the age of 18. Arrighetti (2001) emphasizes the point:

> Now that more libraries offer Internet access and are confronted with the dilemma of using filtering software or restricting children's access to the Internet, an increasing number of libraries will likely institute policies prohibiting unattended children from using the library.

However, latchkey programs can be a positive, integrative force for children in the community if the commitment in terms of staff time, financial resources and program planning is made and evaluations kept. Homework assistance centers in public libraries, for example, increase attendance and are appropriate for community outreach. Many public libraries see the potential for programs for latchkey children to be a valuable marketing tool in that they bring youth to the forefront in terms of community responsibility. Arrighetti states that such an acceptance of after-school services for children also benefits special services for young adults in terms of how the existing spaces within the library are being used. In

Students look to the library for inspiration

(Photo by North Georgia Media. Courtesy Shutterstock 2007.)

an article entitled 'Embracing inclusion: the critical role of the library', Briony Train, Pete Dalton and Judith Elkin (2000) state that research conducted by the University of Central England demonstrated the capacity of the public library service to combat the exclusion of the child from society by enabling access to the adult world. The paper concludes that the public library service supports the educational, social, and cultural development of all citizens, and that the public library is the essence of an inclusive institution for families and children. The principle of inclusion addresses the need for the public library to be flexible. Mae Benne (1991: 245) writes 'The strength of the public library for children is that they are free to use its services as individuals, and as members of a classroom or family.' Moreover: 'Children who use the library as a safe haven after school need a sympathetic staff who operate with a clear policy that sets for the behavior expected.' The Milanof-Schlock Library in Mount Joy, Lancaster County, Pennsylvania, provides a daytime shelter and voluntary work for latchkey children when school is out. The library also serves as a community center, senior center and youth center, as the area does not hold these separate facilities (Berry, 2006). According to Cindy Mediavilla (2001), library homework centers 'position the library as a major player in furthering family values, create opportunities to partner with schools, civic groups, and others and help to nurture the next generation of library users.' Today Live Homework Help libraries offer online homework help in over 1,000 library sites across from Alaska to Florida. Urban, suburban, and rural libraries report that providing this online service to middle schoolers and teenagers is a great benefit for the library and the community. Support for latchkey children is philosophically part of the missionary instinct of youth services as it is across organizations such as schools and across educational agencies at the state and national level. The major barrier to cooperation has been identified as a lack of communication between public and school library sectors. The common goals of public and school libraries have been acknowledged for over 40 years. In 1966, Sara Fenwick wrote:

> Both school and public library will be responsible for learning that will span lifetimes, and the education of children will be only the beginning. To recognize these developing needs, there must be continuous planning of all community organizations, but especially of schools and public libraries, for this challenging common endeavor. (Fenwick, quoted in Spelman and Kelly, 2004: 5)

The Yarra-Melbourne Regional Library Corporation in Australia is working to develop positive partnerships and 'achieve better learning outcomes' for young people. In their article entitled 'In visible light: illuminating partnerships across libraries to facilitate lifelong learning for young people', Spelman and Kelly (2004) note:

> With expanding library service development, the time has come to formalize a framework for cooperation between the education and information sectors to ensure the evolution of a cooperative and comprehensive library services for young people. In Queensland, the development of a Smart Library Network which includes the State Library of Queensland, the public library sector, Alia (Australian Library and Information Association) Children's and Youth Services, and the education sector is already helping to facilitate an integrated network of both physical and virtual community spaces which creatively link diverse groups to information, knowledge and each other.

Partnerships such as the Smart Library Network clarify the fact that the tax money which funds both school and public libraries have the potential and responsibility to work for the common good. Collaboration requires commitment and willingness to make a contribution to literacy for youth. The US Library Services and Technology Act of 1997 outlined areas for cooperation between public and school libraries. These included promoting library services that give users access to information through state, regional, national and international electronic networks, promoting services that serve people of diverse geographic, cultural and socio-economic background regardless of disabilities, functional literacy or information skills, and advocating the planning and development of collections cooperatively (Spelman and Kelly, 2004: 8).

Reference interview with children

When speaking of reference interviews with adults, Joy Greiner (1994) cited Baker and Lancaster (1991: 215): 'The measure of success of an interview is the frequency and quality of exchanges because in a reference interview, the librarian's behavior and knowledge most strongly influence the quality of the information provided.' Similarly, the children's librarian's behavior and knowledge can positively influence the frequency and quality of the conversational exchange of information with children and their caregivers. This conversational exchange is based on many environmental cues. Bishop and Salveggi (2001) discuss the stages of child development as a focus for the youth service reference interview technique. Because children from ages two to seven are egocentric and believe everyone shares their views, they can simply be directed to the shelves to find the types of books they like to read. Although the child is not yet ready to access information via the catalogue, the librarian can make suggestions using topical areas of interest, such as animals or television tie-ins. Because computer-searching techniques are mathematically logical, the child may not see the relevance of mathematics to information retrieval. Similarly, classification according to the Dewey Decimal System is an area of mathematical subsets. However, children at this age enjoy searching through images in the interface of the computer catalog and can ask the librarian for help in locating the area of interest. Youth services librarians may adjust the vocabulary they use to inquire if the child's needs have been met since the listening patterns of children through the key stages correspond with cognitive models of child development. Concrete-operational children, ages 7–11, can contemplate cause and effect. As Bishop and Salveggi (2001: 355) explain, 'If a child at this age level wants to learn to play baseball, he or she will be able to think of possible ways to learn that sport – observe others playing baseball, ask questions about baseball, or look for a book that explains the sport.' This ability enhances the child's communication with the librarian. A more mature child will benefit from the encouragement given by the librarian when the appropriate resource has been found. When a child is looking for print resources to help with homework and such subject area resources are unavailable, the librarian can assist by providing a form which alerts the child's teacher to the fact that the child did search for print information on the homework topic. The librarian can also help the child to search for homework resources cited on the Internet as well. Developing paper or online forms to keep track of these types of reference and service activities offered and measuring the success of the materials in answering can be determined by outcomes. The demonstrated information needs of children can be benchmarked and used to determine future possibilities in service.

It is clear that youth services librarians need to view the child in a multidimensional way, beyond considerations of the psychological stage associated with age. The child may not speak English well, or may come from a disadvantaged background. Service to such children may take a bit more time and consideration, and it may involve negotiating the reference interview with a concerned parent as well as with the child. It is important to keep the goal in mind, that the child and parent will continue to make visits to the public library, because through frequent visits to their public library, children may come to see the library as a place to satisfy their curiosity through 'what happens' in books and socialize with their parents, siblings and friends. By listening to the children speak, children's librarians are encouraging their communication skills. Such skills offer the keys to internalization, a concept Lev Vygotsky interpreted as a transformation of social activities into mental activities. The naturalistic method of assisting children in the public library holds the most potential for a positive experience. Even though librarians are usually quick to suggest the source from which the answer to the question might be obtained, it is more effective to clarify the question from the child prior to identifying where the answer might be found.

Serving young adults

The ability to communicate with young adults is a basic characteristic of young adult librarianship. Respecting the dignity of young adults by empathizing with their questioning is important. The impersonal and informal protocols of face-to-face reference engagement used by the librarian with adults is often not appropriate with a teen's communication style. While analysing virtual online reference interviews with teens, Virginia Walter and Cindy Mediavilla found that the chat discourse environment to be so familiar to teens that they recreated this informal environment when asking reference questions online. In turn, librarians used the impersonal, formal protocols of the face-to-face reference encounter. As a result of their experiences, young adults may not perceive the need for having a special librarian assist them. However, 'Where the scholar takes his work seriously, the young person in pursuit of answers to his or her homework assignment fails (or is failed by others) to think of his work as an important endeavor' (Rovenger, 1983). Clearly, librarians have special responsibilities toward young people, who usually have two types of questions, those based on school assignments and those initiated personally.

In 1979 Downey wrote that the majority of public library directors interviewed indicated that expansion of personalized and focused service to this age group was desirable (Downey, 1979); however, the number of young adult specialists serving teens has not increased in twenty years (see US National Center for Education Statistics). More young adults use the library than any other age group, for school assignments, for personal, leisure and vocational reading, as well as for non-book library materials and the Internet. The recognition that the needs of young adults are just as complex as those of adults assists the librarian in the reference interview and in making the library a hospitable and inclusionary place. Sympathetic interaction with young adult patrons in this exploratory period of their lives can make the difference between whether the information available will be used or not. In his report on the 'The First National Survey of Services and Resources for Young Adults in Public Libraries' conducted by the National Center for Education Statistics in 1988 Chelton (1989) noted that, according to the survey, adolescents were using the public library most frequently after school hours and for school-related reasons. Today young adults are still using the public library for school-related reasons, and using the Internet constantly for research, just as they used the library in the 1960s for homework assignments. Nevertheless, regardless of cyberspace, the idea of the public library as an alternative environment for young adults continues to have merit because of the importance of interacting with peers in a safe place. Young adult rooms tend to include encyclopedias (such as the Merit Encyclopedia), English literature, YA fiction, popular magazines, classics, and award-winning science fiction. Compact disks of music are available, a meeting room, catalog and Internet access, and career information. Use of the public library by young adults is motivated by the resources available, such as booklists, a job board, crisis information hotlines, specialized programming and activities, a popular materials collection, a game room, and Internet access. Judith Flum (1983) described the importance of disseminating personal crisis information and promoting resources which address topics from sex to drugs to coping as ways to help teenagers survive adolescence and thrive as lifelong learners and users of libraries in the future.

Programming for children

Events and activities scheduled for children in public libraries are available via schedules and calendars posted on library websites. Baby Time, Toddler Time, Story Time, Craft Time and Family Story Time are sessions commonly held for parents or caregivers and their children. Magic Shows, Reptile Adventures and Book Buddies programs are also offered. Using the web page, library patrons can click on the underlined event title to register. They can also display their personal schedule to see the events for which they are currently signed up.

Public library websites feature gateways such as the Internet Public Library for Homework Help. Online tools such as dictionaries, thesauri, almanacs, encyclopedias, quotations, and atlases are available on many public library websites. Help with history, mathematics and current events is offered through hypertext resources as well as the *Ask a Librarian* telephone number and e-mail address. Bibliographic style manuals and general suggestions for research and writing are also given.

Practitioners need to measure their success in collection

strength (including access to databases) and the success of programming activities to determine how relevant such services are.

Currently, outcome-based assessment is recommended. Success can be measured through the evaluation of storytime experiences (maintaining a reflective, online journal of materials used and the children's responses to the material). If permission from parents is obtained prior to conducting research on the story time experience, and the children's identities are held confidential, a qualitative software program can be a thematic tool, providing insight into the practitioner's success. Children's librarians can measure the growth of vocabulary, socialization skill development, and the success of their resources (books, puppets, finger plays, string plays, music and dance) and other resources available in handbooks on storytelling to engage children. Communication with parents regarding their children's literacy development is perhaps the most rewarding aspect of children's librarianship. Inter-generational programming activities also carry this reward. Young adults vote with their feet. If they are fortunate enough to live in a public library community where a young adult librarian is employed, the measure of how successful the program is can be determined by measuring the attitudes and perceptions of young adults, and their awareness of the resources available to them.

Virginia Walter (2003) points out the fact that summer reading programs, book discussion opportunities, and marketing are all value-based practices. The theoretical foundations of summer reading programs, book discussion opportunities, and the marketing of the programs themselves all fall within the service value imperative. Youth services librarians address the acquisition of language across the 'practice' board. Adele Fasick states:

> Despite the many changes in technology, children still need to experience the world through all of their senses. They should not only listen to nursery rhymes and fairy tales, they should mark the rhythm with their hands, walk through the journeys with their feet, act out the stories with their bodies, and create their reactions with crayon, paints, and music. Librarians should consider the value of varied experiences when others talk about computers satisfying all of children's information needs. (Fasick, 1998: xvi)

Because preschool children learn with their entire bodies, concepts such as up and down and under and over are said to be critical to the acquisition of related language. By drawing (or scribbling), young children learn cause and effect, and pretend play can help children practise social interaction (Feinberg et al., 1998).

Children's librarians practise nurturing literacy as an ethical stand. They communicate to the children and young adults that they are valued. They provide their audience with a wide range of reading materials and believe in giving them the freedom to choose what they want to read – this freedom is a mental concept of the social environment they encounter. Focus groups are used with young adults to discover services which work well and services which might be implemented in the future. This schematic for understanding intellect dates back to the Swiss psychologist Jean Piaget. His description of the activities of assimilation and accommodation describe the thought process as a change in mental models where adaptation occurs and a broader range of experiences becomes available to the youth. One child's experience of a story will be somewhat different to another's because each is interpreting the experience through their own 'thought world'. Brazleton

(1992) wrote that emotional development is the basis for future cognitive success. If a child develops a good sense of himself and of his competence in all areas, he will be ready to acquire cognitive competence later on. Clearly, examining relevant research in reading can also serve as the basis for the development of improved library services to children.

The years from six to eight clearly are years of rapid development. Children's librarians can model library use to children and their parents and encourage a connection to the library. Traditional children's services share this timeless social accommodation mission, even in the Digital Age. Books and reading are still keys to lifelong learning, and computers and technology are unlikely to replace books and reading in the education of young children for a variety of reasons. Although electronic technology is a better medium to convey information that is largely factual and conveys understanding through better graphical displays, print imparts knowledge in a more personal way than do computers, and provides the basic intellectual context for processing information – the context of narrative (Quek and Higgins, 2003). The experience of identifying with the main character of a book deepens the child's comprehension and enjoyment of the story. Helen Keller described this process in 1903:

> Children who hear acquire language without any particular effort; the words that fall from others' lips they catch on the wing, as it were, delightedly, while the little deaf child must trap them by a slow and often painful process. But whatever the process, the result is wonderful. Gradually from naming an object we advance step by step until we have traversed the vast distance between our first stammered syllable and

the sweep of thought in a line of Shakespeare. (From The Story of My Life, 1903 – see: *http://www .worldwideschool.org/library/books/hst/biography/St oryofMyLife/chap7.html*)

Teaching children how to use the catalog to locate their reading material helps them become field-independent learners, as gleaning information from websites is also important in the growth of the intellect.

The concept of emergent literacy is now used to describe literacy processes that occur in the family circle and during traditional storytime presentations in the public library. What children learn about reading and writing prior to actually being able to read or write is a powerful motivator of literacy. Organized programs such as those of Family Place, the Literary Network Committee and Motheread (see Fiore, 2005) encourage engagement with babies, toddlers and preschoolers in public libraries and, of course, build up the relationship with the parents. Children learn how to attend to language by interacting and modeling others in the environment. For example, if a child 'models' holding a book and babbling as if reading, this behavior is considered emergent literacy. If a child repeats rhymes and fingerplays conducted in story time, this is also considered emergent literacy. Although emergent literacy is the term for such early literacy activity, the idea is not new – story times in public libraries have existed for over a hundred years. Teachers may have slightly different perceptions of how story time can assist readers: According to Barbara K. Gunn et al. (2006):

Children learn about print from a variety of sources and in the process come to realize that print – not pictures – carries the story. They also learn how text is structured visually (i.e., text begins at the top of the page, moves from left to right, and carries over to the next page when it is turned). While knowledge about the convention of print enables children to understand the physical structure of language, the conceptual knowledge that printed words convey a message also helps children bridge the gap between oral and written language.

Children up to about six years of age are learning letter and number discrimination, recognition and scanning, as well as the rudiments of reading (e.g. the ability to recognize their own names and a few words).

Children's librarians in public libraries emphasize the recreational approach to listening and interacting with

Young adults visiting the stacks (*c.*1960s)

(Reproduced courtesy of the Hemet Public Library Local History Collection.)

literature rather than a strategic intervention with the written word, which emergent literacy implies. Story time for preschoolers involves social learning – learning to be part of a group, learning how to listen and engaging in the activities modeled by the librarian. Story time is an acclimation process. The design of such sessions is not school-based as much as it is based on the social context of family and community as support for literacy. Perhaps this too is a gender issue. Christine Pawley states, 'It is important to remember that the strongest historical association between gender and the library science curriculum is between women instructors and children's literature and services' (2005: 301)

The importance of observing adolescent behavior in the attempt to serve adolescents appropriately is often brought up in the library literature. Barbara Combes writes that the 'Net Generation' (the term was coined by Donald Tapscott to describe those born after 1985) demonstrate 'a different culture of use when using and seeking information delivered electronically' and that 'they have never known a world without instantaneous communication and easy access to vast quantities of information using multiple formats, text types, graphics and multimedia' (2006: 401). Still, competency in the application of technology to homework or everyday problems may open up reference interview techniques for young adult librarians because for the Net Generation, the primary use of the Internet is for communication and entertainment. Multi-user online communities based on video games provide visualizations referred to by Joel Foreman (2003) as 'immersive worlds' and are channeled as 'edutainment' programs for interactive learning.

Outside of entertainment, however, basic information technology skills may not translate into competent information handling skills as the nature of the Internet is chaotic. Finding the right balance of entertainment as well as assistance with homework is the challenge. It's important to remember that reading in adolescence is an emotional experience. Because information-seeking addresses the affective domain of adolescence Shenton (2003) wrote of the tendency of young people to use the most accessible information sources first. Subject-specialized databases may pose a problem. Even young adults who are proficient in seeking information on the Internet and through electronic databases may rarely question the authenticity of the information. Their burgeoning independence may prevent them from asking for help because they are reluctant to admit to lack of knowledge. Young adult librarians cannot assume that young adults have the skills to find information using electronic resources even if they are quite proficient at games. Information density is a problem. Combes cited the UK Joint Information Systems Committee Report which found that there is an overwhelming reliance by academics and students on Internet search engines rather than on the use of specialized electronic information services or the deep Web (2006: 404). Everhart and Valenza (2004) question whether young adults are ignoring valuable print resources and whether they are settling for low-quality information because high-quality information requires more time and effort to find. Negative stereotypes of librarians by young adults can prevent the benefit of human guidance in planning, processing, and thinking about resources. According to Everhart and Valenza:

> Well after they leave our classrooms, students will be making information decisions. Which car should I buy? How much should I pay for it? Which political candidates will best represent me? How can I convince

the school board we need a special program? How do I persuade the corporate board to accept my proposal?' (2004: 55)

Young adults thrive in an atmosphere of social learning and mutual engagement with families. If the public library positions itself as a comfortable community for young adults, they might attend programs, form advisory boards and begin asking questions about how to retrieve and use information effectively as well as how to meet one another, contribute, and value the librarian. Traditional booklists of popular reading for young adults still have a place for their convenience and portability and because young adult literature addresses problems encountered in adolescence.

Marketing the public library as an inclusive space for teenagers will take the insight of a reflective practitioner with input from her young adult audience. Just as in adult services, popular marketing tools are print catalogs, flyers, and reviews. Librarians, publishers, and vendors all rate web-based catalogs and databases as highly successful marketing tools in all library awareness endeavors (Belanger, 2002).

Programming for young adults

Public library programming for young adults and collection services to them in general were first conceived as an alternative to school-based pursuits. Recreational reading in the form of romance, hobbies, comics, science fiction, and Japanese anime is very popular in the 11–18 age range. Role-playing computer games for young adults take the form of complex fantasies. Specific collection provision for this developmental time of life has only been in place for 40 years, beginning with the publication of *The Outsiders* by S.E. Hinton in 1967. Programs for young adults focus on reading for pleasure and enrichment, and social and cultural competence, and the input of young adults is essential because communicating to them that their opinions matter is part and parcel of gaining such competence. In the article 'Assets and outcomes: new directions in young adult services in public libraries' by Nann Blain Hilyard, as Patrick Jones explains, 'The true mission of our work in libraries with teens emerges to our profession, to our community, and to the teens we serve: our purpose is to help teens thrive and develop into caring, competent adults' (Hilyard, 2002: 199).

Collaboration with media specialists in area schools for shared programming such as book talks and co-hosting author presentations are often successful, and participation by teens in a Teen Advisory Council to assist with children's summer reading programs is welcomed. Young adults can collaborate and contribute with one another through recognition and engagement with an online library newsletter, using the YA home page to respond and write reviews of young adult fiction. Online and paper newsletters can be circulated by the Advisory Board and placed in the schools and public library. Liaison with English departments at the local high schools is strengthened through library holdings of the classics for young adults. A community relations specialist can assist with announcements of programs which are mailed or faxed to local schools.

Jones et al. (2004) are the authors of *Connecting Young Adults and Libraries* while the corresponding web page *http://www.connectingya.com/* features a plethora of recommended summer reading programs for young adults. Program resources, best practices, and a directory of websites for programming ideas can be adapted for the library. The American Library Association's Young Adult Libraries Association (YALSA) (*http://www.ala.org/yalsa/ about/index.html*) offers professional resources and READ posters which have great appeal to young adults. The provision of resources and programs all address the critical need to improve reading skills among youth. Jones advocates the provision of magazines as important tools of collection provision to young adults, and reasons that titles such as *Seventeen* and *YM* (*Young Miss*) are recreational but useful sources of health and self-help information. He states: 'The most current and often most readable information available for teens on sex does not come in books, but in the pages of these magazines' (Jones, 2002: 139). Information on sexuality is sought by young adults in public libraries and should be viewed as a special need. Rebecca Cohen, recipient of the 2006 Frances Henne YALSA Research Award, writes:

> At a time when the United States has the highest rate of teen pregnancy in the developed world and adolescents are contracting HIV faster than any other demographic group in this country, it is more critical than ever for public and private institutions to provide comprehensive sexuality information to young adults. (See: *http://www.ala.org/ala/yalsa/newsandeventsb/ henne.htm*)

The most controversial magazines do not end up in public libraries. Examples of traditional magazines aimed at adults and popular with young adults include *People*, *Glamour*, *Mademoiselle*, *Car and Driver*, *Cosmopolitan* and *Sports Illustrated*. Book review media for young adult resources are available via jobbers such as Baker & Taylor, Ingram and

Bookmen. Publisher's catalogs and the professional periodical published by the American Library Association, *Voice of Youth Advocates* (*VOYA*), are extremely useful. Jones also suggests that the provision of music to YA culture encourages connection with the library, and this connection can be strengthened by the use of non-print media (other than interactive computer sites). He suggests setting up a review committee made up of YAs and using the charts which list top music releases. He also suggests paying attention to what is selling in the marketplace, as young adults want to listen to what other young adults are listening to, set general guidelines and establish a budget (Jones, 2002). CD-ROMs which assist as reference indices and entertainment are important for YAs, and the *Library Journal* reviews many to assist in purchasing decisions. Classics available on tape may serve an educational purpose and be more palatable to a young adult audience. Video/DVD collections can potentially cause reconsideration requests because R-rated videos are commonly restricted to those over 18.

It is important to remember that libraries are not the only source of non-print media, but public libraries maintaining YA print collections often provide a consistent collection source of popular and retrospective literature addressing the experience of adolescence and deal with high-interest topics.

The creation of an evaluation framework for electronic information resources for young women was the joint undertaking of Douglass College's Douglass Project for Rutgers Women in Math, Science, and Engineering and of the Girl Scouts of the USA. Eight evaluation criteria aligned to young women's information-seeking behavior research were recommended as tools of selection: confidence, collaboration, personal identification, contextuality, flexibility/motility, social connectivity, inclusion, and graphic/multimedia concentration. Related questions to consider during resource evaluation were: 'Does the resource use a tone of respect?' 'Does the resource encourage users to explore related topics on their own?' and 'Above all, does the resource support and nurture young women's confidence in themselves and their abilities?' (Douglass College, 2000). Young women prefer to work collaboratively and prefer narrative description as opposed to figures and charts. Graphic and multimedia content of high quality will maintain attention and interest. Resources should depict equal numbers of women and men along with people from many racial and ethnic groups and present marginalized groups in positions of respect and influence. Related questions to consider during resource evaluation are: 'Is the information age-appropriate?' 'Is the information overly simplified or too technical?' 'Is the background knowledge necessary to comprehend much of the content beyond the experience of most young people'?

Technology itself presents the paradox of relationships – one can be liberated by freedom from physical appearance, yet one longs to be physically present – particularly for the young adult. This tension can be related to the experience of getting to know oneself. Personal blogs as online diaries incorporate computers and the Internet, e-mails and chat rooms. Apart from books and literature, pod casting allows users to download radio shows, programs or events onto their computer hard drives and then in turn transfer the file to a portable device. A user can view or listen to live or recorded video or audio via streaming technology, and can rent popular movie downloads online. Ironically, one of the dystopian elements of technology is that the more communication devices which are available, the more impersonal technology becomes. The theme of isolation or existentialism has been part of the young adult experience and often depicted in coming-of-age or survival stories.

Ghost stories are traditionally popular fiction for children and young adults, and today, thematically, ghosts haunt technology. In the article entitled 'Contemporary ghost stories: cyberspace in fiction for children and young adults', Marla Harris stated:

> Despite the presence of dystopian elements, this fiction remains optimistic overall about the potential of technology to connect individuals in positive ways and to create communities modeled on tolerance and inclusion. (2005: 111)

Online anonymity may address the young adult's search for identity in the way survival stories did prior to computer access. The screen identity can alleviate peer pressure. Creating a community modeled on tolerance and inclusion is a mission statement of public librarianship, particularly to children and young adults. If the public library has a special librarian to serve young adults, adolescents are acknowledged as a special service group. This period of life is distinct from childhood and distinct from adulthood and must be serviced by specialized resources and provision.

Developing and maintaining relevant collections for children and young adults

Selection is primarily a 'matching' exercise in that the librarian matches the interests of a certain age group to subjects often appearing in the literature. Selection is an aesthetic task in many ways. Often, one's own view of childhood is reflected in the literature, and certain themes are enduring as universals. The children's librarian, by getting in touch with him or herself as a young reader, listener, and learner, can review books and other information reflectively. Such reflection helps to discern the emotional connections to literature and music that tend to satisfy children too.

More objectively, the stages of the child's and young adult's intellectual and emotional development form the basis for collections as well as programming. Librarians use book reviews to determine appropriate holdings based on the needs of the community – this is what makes the collection relevant. The collection policy is the key to collecting materials which appeal to preschoolers, beginning readers, school students and young adults. Resources in electronic format, such as DVDs and software, can be collected which support the goals of the collection. Although a controversial topic, the collection development policy is often applicable to both print and electronic resources. Print resources are foundational to young readers. The Internet can be extremely useful to them for recreational sites and for use in homework assignment preparation if they are assisted in information evaluation.

Story times given by children's librarians link the illustrations in picture books to the action in the story, and collecting for the storytelling aspect of librarianship is important. Children begin to associate text, familiar words and phonics (letter sounds) with pictures. They develop the ability to use structural clues ('what word sounds right in this sentence?') and context clues ('what word makes sense here?') to read unfamiliar words. A child who cannot read yet tells the story by the pictures of a picture book or by memorizing the shape of text on the page is 'reading.' Such a child has developed a strategy to understand and delight in the book. This stage is critical and parents and librarians need to be able to provide children with appropriate books so that they can develop and refine these strategies along with their likes and dislikes. Books that support such strategies have the following characteristics: illustrations that closely reflect the words; familiar, predictable, repetitive language patterns that might have a rhythm or rhyme; primarily simple (but not controlled) vocabulary; and a clear, concise and interesting storyline. Such stories have appealed to children for generations. Often children perplex their caregivers by insisting that a book be read repeatedly. The colors, shapes, cadence, tone or storyline in the book are particularly appealing to the child and this wish should be granted. Wish fulfillment is said to be a conventional cornerstone of children's literature (as is an adventure away from parents).

One should not underestimate the power of humor in children's and young adult books. Children enjoy laughing at situations they can readily identify with, and so do adolescents. Both audiences enjoy the absurd and have a good sense of irony as expressed by tone. Poetry, for example, often elicits very personal responses in both children and young adults, and a selection of poetry should be available for all age groups. Nursery rhymes, jump-rope skipping rhymes, fold poems, lyric poems, nonsense verse, and narrative poems are foundational to the collection. Library programming which addresses online poetry writing for adolescents can be encouraged through the library's website.

The development of empathy in the reader is perhaps the most important aspect of work with children. Children can benefit from stories than explain what life is like for people restricted by handicaps, politics, or circumstance, or whose lives are different from theirs because of culture or geography. Often, story characters are placed in situations

The library offers a student a place for contemplation

(Photo by Andres Rodriquez. Courtesy Shutterstock 2007.)

that require them to make moral decisions. By middle childhood, readers can naturally consider what they would do in such a situation. As the story unfolds and the character's decision and the consequences of that choice are disclosed, readers discover whether their own decisions would have had positive outcomes. Regular experience with these types of stories can help young people formulate their own concepts of right and wrong.

Another valuable result of children interacting with literature is that they quickly come to recognize the literary and artistic styles of many authors and illustrators. This is an important step to literacy awareness – that is to recognize that the style of one writer or illustrator differs from another, and that a piece of writing or an illustration has personal appeal. Children who read regularly from a wide variety of children's books soon develop their own personal preferences for types of books and select favorite authors and illustrators. Teachers and librarians have long recognized the motivational potential of personal preference and interest as expressed through self-selection of reading materials. They also know that the more children read and the greater the variety of literature they read, the more discerning readers they become. The more children know about their world, the more they discover things about themselves – who they are, what they value, and what they stand for. These personal insights alone are sufficient to warrant making books an essential part of any child's home and school experience. Literature is valuable for its academic benefits, as school achievers are also readers. Teens rated reading higher in importance in terms of its impact on future success than math, science, and computers (Peter D. Hart Research Associates, 2001). If children and young adults are unable to independently access the knowledge and information embedded in books and other printed materials that are part of the curriculum, they cannot achieve to their potential intellectual ability. However, the value of the Internet as a venue of student writing cannot be denied.

Strategies for creating a community of literate young adults include: creating a library space that draws teenagers; advocating for free reading time during the school day; extending the reading community through programs, inviting teenagers to read; providing young adults with strategies for understanding academic texts; and inviting young adults to write (Hughes-Hassell and Mancall, 2005). In dealing with young adults on a personal level, Margaret Edwards suggests:

> Don't play favorites or encourage sentimental attachments. Cordial relationships should be built as

far as possible on a mutual pleasure in reading. Don't impose an opinion. Let the teenager think his thoughts and feel free to express them. Don't conclude a book is popular because it circulates. In the discussion of a book recently read, the librarian has an opportunity to develop in young people sharper critical faculties and a better basis for enjoyment and to introduce to them new and related fields of reading. (1969: 29)

There is a direct causal relationship between early literacy-related activities in the home and the child's language development, so in many ways, the mother of the child being 'the child's first teacher' is undeniably valid. Story time in the public library enriches the child's experience with language, and strengthens the cultural connection between the home, public library and school community. Zweizig (1993) described public libraries as a place of opportunity for preschoolers to learn, and this is a popular and well-documented role. Children's responses to literature can begin very early in life. Gunn et al. (2006) write: 'Experiences with print (through reading and writing) give preschool children an understanding of the conventions, purpose, and function of print – understandings that have been shown to play an integral part in learning to read.' The conversational dimension of reading and writing is significant in work with children and young adults and is based on the power of narrative. Positive interaction with children and books is necessary so that information can be used to the advantage of human relations. Children's librarians internalize the mission of building positive human relations through their work as an ethical and professional stance of librarianship as a whole. As we have seen, Ismail Abdullahi cites Natalia Tyulina, former Director of the Dag Hammarskjold Library:

We live in a time when significant efforts are made by different countries, nations, and peoples toward better understanding of each other, the knowledge that mutual understanding is the most important condition for maintaining peace in the world. As technology acts as a cultural eraser, librarianship serves an increasingly important role, bringing together the records of the best achievement of humanity and the individual human being, thus helping to establish better understanding among people. In this respect our profession may be considered one of the 'peace-keeping tools.' (See *http://darkwing.uroregon.edu/~felsing/ala/abdullahi.html*)

From concept books to the young adult novel

Many concept books do not teach concepts in the way that a lot of adults believe they can. These books are meant for preschoolers and their content is based on topics such as the alphabet, colors, shapes, and counting. Concept books are better used as tools for supplementing and reinforcing direct experiences, not as substitutes for direct experience. However, as regards literacy, concept books may serve as a vehicle for ritualized dialog, also known as expansion. By providing concept books, the parent also provides the framework for verbal dialog. Picture book reading also has the structure of dialog. As an infant the child communicates by smiling, reaching, pointing, and babbling vocalizations, and the mother interprets these with labels for objects. Similarly, an increase in the storyteller's 'expansions' is related to an increase in the children's spontaneous imitations. Their engagement with the story is deepened. Jean Piaget labeled this stage of development as 'preoperational.' Children under the age of seven tend to base knowledge on perception. As children grow, their knowledge comes to be based on perception as well as deduction, and they can ponder cause and effect. The incidental learning which occurs as the children listen to the conversations of adults and other children around them helps them begin to understand their environment in a powerful way. The 'ritualized dialog' technique practised by the storyteller is best done in a rereading of the story. A response activity from the children need not occur as silence is a worthy response to the book as well. Ann Carlson (1991) suggests in the *Preschooler and the Library* that

Children waiting in line to check out books (c.1960s)

(Reproduced courtesy of the Hemet Public Library Local History Collection.)

activities designed solely to teach the alphabet or numbers are much less appropriate than providing a print-rich environment that stimulates language. A preschooler who comes from a home where books, magazines, and newspapers are read and where conversations are held has a head start in language engagement because they are immersed in the tools of narrative. A child who is perceived as an emergent reader by family and caregivers is likely to live up to this expectation.

Beginning readers are meant for children to read themselves. These books often use rhyme and colorful and amusing illustrations to carry the plot. Non-fiction beginning readers and autobiographical beginning readers are gaining in popularity and feature photographs of children and the communities in which they live. Series fiction and non-fiction for children can be used for pleasure reading and homework. Children's librarians can compile a 'kit' of information for the teacher to check out for the classroom when students are composing reports. School districts may maintain a circulating collection which is centralized for such a purpose. Although the public library may limit the amount of non-fiction books a child can check out on the same topic, the children's librarians may order more selections based on the topic to meet future needs. One of the most significant benefits of technology in building literacy is the story-writing software available to children. Richly illustrated, animated postcards can be sent via e-mail.

Adolescents have needs and concerns distinct from either children or young adults. Young adult literature may address controversial topics appropriate for an adolescent contemplating his or her identity. Young adult literature may not appeal until the child has reached the age of abstract reasoning at about 11. At this age, the emerging adolescent begins to contemplate the morality of specific choices in life, as the characters in young adult novels often undergo hardships and, consequently, profound moral growth. Research is needed to explore the significance of reading for pleasure in the life of teens so that public libraries can serve and market recreational reading selections. Because of the vast array of multimedia options available to the twenty-first century teenager, integrating books and reading into the technology available, i.e. computer games, the Internet, and friends in an online chat room, is the challenge for the young adult librarian. Even though teens may sense the potential power of reading in their lives, often there is little time to read for pleasure in a highly structured school day. How well the provision of service and resources is promoted to teens can provide a marketing goal.

An exploratory survey of 159 teens in Nova Scotia conducted by Vivian Howard (2006) revealed that the book reading gap between the genders appears to be widening as teenage girls in Nova Scotia read significantly more fiction books than their male counterparts while boys are much more likely to be readers of non-fiction books. This gender gap is not apparent for newspapers or magazines. Peers are perceived to be influential in reading choices whereas librarians are not. However, as Howard states:

> Although teens may not recognize the influence of librarians on their reading choices, any teen who uses the public library for leisure reading material is, of course, being influenced indirectly by book displays, book lists, and the very collection itself – all of which reflect the professional activity and selection decisions made by librarians. (2006: 6)

Teens are often not aware of library websites and school–library cooperation can be enhanced through publicizing such facilities. Howard states that the Opening Doors study recommended that libraries 'solicit preteens' opinions about library services and collections through focus groups, an advisory board or ideas team and website surveys or polls' (2006: 7). Many boys who identify themselves as reluctant readers may instead be reading magazines, comics, or websites, so the scope of recreational reading for teens has broadened.

An active young adult advisory group may be presented with the opportunity to write a book, journal or website review using an online newsletter sponsored by their public library. This newsletter can be posted in the local high school. Members of the advisory group may be invited to participate in library board meetings which address services and problems. Contemporary newspapers and magazines of interest to young adults need to be available in the library because they have a normative effect. Because individuals who borrow from the public library buy more books than those who do not, partnerships between libraries and bookstores can increase the market for buying and borrowing within the community. Andrew Albanese (2006) quotes Ben Vershbow as follows:

> Soon, books will literally have discussions inside of them, both live chats and asynchronous exchanges through comments and social annotation. You will be able to see who else out there is reading that book and be able to open up a dialog with them.

Authors of popular fiction often have an autobiographical blog which offers interaction and discussion of their novels in chat rooms. The dimension of communication with the author and the personal depth afforded by the blog (web log) is appealing to young adults because it gives them an opportunity to voice their opinions and be heard by their peers. Such writing capability should be capitalized upon by the youth services librarian. Award-winning authors of young adult novels welcome the input of their young readers and teens enjoy the social networking possibilities available to them. A bibliography of popular sites can be offered in the booklist distributed by the young adult librarian. Of course, the booklist will have to be updated as blog sites change, and print material is more convenient.

Pre-readers

In general, pre-readers rather than older children are thought more successful as a picture book audience for several reasons: they still believe in fantasy, they hold images in awe, even when they do not move, and they are curious about visual images as symbols. Since their verbal language is more limited, they are more intuitive rather than literal. They are empathetic rather than self-conscious and are innocent rather than experienced. Pre-readers also are just beginning to grasp the notions of sequencing and connotation as well as expression in words as well as pictures. Use of picture books with pre-readers often competes well against electronic visuals because the book's format can be enjoyed at leisure; it is an object that can be used effectively to teach as well as entertain.

Favorite concrete experiences depicted in picture books are themes about family, community interdependence, the use of tools, nature, animals and wild creatures, celebrations, play and fantasy. Some of the conventions of picture book illustrations are the repetition of images, the protagonist's place in the picture paralleling his or her purpose in the story, and the inclusion of decorative endpapers to add a sense of place to the illustrations.

Other aspects of book selection

Book selection is often determined by the parameters of the collection development policy which in turn is based on the community served. With the advent of online resources, selecting children's books in accordance with journal reviews has never been easier. The basic principles of book selection involve an examination of genre, theme, characterization, setting, plot and style, and the place of the selection within the collection. If possible, award winners and classics are automatically ordered.

The Children's Literature Comprehensive Database (*http://www.childrenslit.com*) provides an outstanding and international source of aggregated reviews for PreK to Grade 12 (preschoolers to secondary school) media. More than 30 review sources and more than 300,000 reviews represent multiple viewpoints. Links to author/illustrator web resources and interviews are available. The *ALAN Review, ARBA, Audio File, Booklist, Bulletin of the Center for Children's Books, CCBC Choices, Children's Literature, Horn Book Guide, KIRKUS Reviews, KLIATT, Recorded Books, Resource Links, Science Books and Films, VOYA* and others are featured. Reviews from *Books for Keeps*, the UK's magazine about the children's books industry, are included as well as reviews from *Resource Links, Canadian Review of Materials* (Canada), *Inis* (Ireland) and *Lollipops – What's on for Kids* (Australia). The database also meets the needs of university librarians, professors, and university students as a resource for assignments. The database can help classroom teachers access curriculum tools, reading guides and lesson plans for children and young adults.

The key elements of review sources are that they provide the citation information needed for purchase, summaries are brief and factual, a genre classification is given, the criticism notes potential uses, strengths, and weaknesses, a rating scheme is included, and recommendations are given as to audience, type of library, subject, controversy, and uses. There are four types of review sources: notification sources (such as *Publisher's Weekly*), evaluative sources (such as *Library Journal* and *School Library Journal*), popular sources (such as *Kirkus Reviews* and the *New York Times Book Review*), and comparative or scholarly sources (such as the *Multicultural Review*). Library sources have a selection focus, employing the use of bibliographies (subject, fiction, age/grade level, award lists, best lists) and union lists (such as the National Union Catalog (NUC)) and the current review sources noted. Publisher sources have marketing as their focus. Those with close ties to publishers are *Books in Print* and the *Bowker Annual*. The *Publisher's Trade List Annual* is direct from the publishers and *Publisher's Weekly* along with many catalogs and brochures are promotional rather than evaluative. The aesthetic character of the picture book format cannot be overlooked. A book with many pictures may be eye-catching for lower and middle-graders, but the type may be too large and the reading level too low at seventh grade. One must look at the merits of a selection in terms of 'fit' to the population served. Controversies such as the appropriateness of fairy tales and comics for a child audience, the concern that children will experience fear while reading fantasy literature, the depiction of alternative lifestyles, the inclusion of classics and so on are age old disputes and most probably cannot be resolved. Selection should be criterion-based in terms of the strength of the elements of literature

The beauty and power of the written word is a constant

(Photo by Juriah Mosin. Courtesy Shutterstock 2007.)

present, the age appropriateness, whether there are positive reviews and the need for a balanced collection, one which serves the family or one which serves the school curriculum. There is also a need for ephemera. However, avoiding controversial selections simply on the basis that the resource will be challenged is censorship.

Picture books rely on the conventions of illustration and design – artistic elements such as line, color, light and dark, shape, space, and texture. Response to color and color harmony is recognized to reflect personal preferences more than any of the other elements – it may do so for the children's librarian. The cover or jacket of picture books is like a poster that reflects mood, text, and artistic style.

Considerations of value in book selection would apply to materials in other formats.

Beyond general considerations are the specific strengths and limitations of the materials. The website Kidsource (*http://www.kidsource.com/books/fs/f.books.to.build.on .html*) suggests that the following points be kept in mind when selecting for a family audience:

- Does the publication, video or audio cassette take into account implicit and explicit assumptions, beliefs or values that are appropriate or potentially problematic for the receiving family? Is the information presented in a format preferred by the receiving family? For example, if a family's preferred mode of accessing information is through oral or visual means, is the information you are providing available in audio or video versions?

- Is the literacy level appropriate for the receiving family? For example, is the information organized and presented in a way that a family member with fewer than six years of schooling can benefit? Or is the information presented in such a way that the family will find the material patronizing?

- Are technical terms and jargon explained effectively? For example, does the publication include a glossary of frequently used terms?

- Are diverse groups of people represented in the images? Do the images suggest a contemporary or non-stereotypical view of various families? Material that portrays people of all cultures and both genders in positive ways are much sought after in book selection for children. The purpose of stock is to help children expand their knowledge by discovery of common experiences and to encourage them to read for enjoyment. They can grow to understand their own and other people's situations, and in doing so develop emotionally as well as intellectually.

Use of children's services should be extended to adults caring for children, and this will have implications for the children's librarian. Knowledge of child development in terms of how a child acquires the skills of listening, talking, reading, and writing, and an awareness of how children cope with new experiences, are important for the children's librarian, because relevant books and information can contribute to a parent's ability to support children in their educational and life growth.

The audience of the underserved in public library services is a complex one. For example, Ann Curry (2005) notes that a good reference librarian can mean the difference between gay or lesbian youth fleeing the library or considering the library a helpful refuge. Curry noted that although many librarians maintain the confidentiality of reference questions, an awareness of gay or lesbian books as well as current web resources is needed.

Multicultural selections

Denise Agosto (2006) described five major characteristics which can serve as evaluation criteria for multicultural selections: accuracy, expertise, respect, purpose, and quality. The selector should ask a series of questions based on these characteristics as portrayals which are inaccurate tend to perpetuate stereotypes. Cultural aspects – for example, food, dress, and setting – should be portrayed accurately, and individuals should be featured as individuals in appearance. Non-English words should be spelled and used correctly, and historical information needs to be accurate. In multicultural literature the authors and illustrator need to demonstrate expertise in their portrayal of the culture, and such expertise may be related to research or direct experience. Bias in the portrayal of characters and cultural setting is not acceptable because it is not respectful. Since biased communication relies on stereotypical assumptions and attitudes expressed in language and applied to a group, the selector should be able to see the work as of high quality independent of its multicultural status. Language and imagery that is inclusive of a diversity of backgrounds and experience is an important teaching tool and reflective of purpose. Using inclusive communication is one way to achieve equality of opportunity in our society. Any community that has a variety of lifestyles based on different sexual preferences and inclusive language will reflect that fact. Any discussion of issues pertaining to sexual orientation should be accurate and informed. Lesbians and gay men should be described in terms that do not demean or trivialize them or encourage distorted images of their experience and lives. It is also sometimes common to describe people with disabilities in a way that emphasizes the disability over the person, for example paraplegics, the blind, the schizophrenic. Yet most people do not think of themselves in this way. To write instead of a child who has impaired mobility puts this characteristic into the perspective of a much wider life experience, even for a child.

Reading and reading programs

Many states coordinate an annual statewide vacation or summer reading program that encourages recreational reading for children and families. Family literacy activities are highlighted and parents are encouraged to participate in the program with their children. Booklogs, game boards, bookmarks, posters, and stickers are designed to help promote the program in each of the public library facilities in the state. Face-to-face meetings for children's librarians are held in the spring for the purpose of sharing potential programs for the statewide summer reading program. Areas of focus at these meetings are funding opportunities and help with grants, the national Prime Time Family Reading Time Program, and how to maintain a performer's directory and a professional collection. Official websites explaining the program, information and resource kits, and program pilot information hyperlinks are available. A children's listserv address, public service announcement downloads, sticker designs, bibliographies, files of stories which can be heard online and the service manual which covers common questions are also available for download (see, for example, Georgia Public Library Services website).

Teenagers are encouraged to volunteer at the library, and the website features futuristic graphics. The Teen Vacation Reading Program site for Alabama, Virginia, South Carolina and Georgia (*http://www.teenreading.com*) is supported by the Institute of Library Services under the provisions of the Library Services and Technology Act (LSTA) 1996 as administered by the various state library agencies.

Outside of summer reading programs and storytelling, family-centered programming has the most potential to create readers and frequent users of the public library. Not all children will have substantial home libraries to consult, and the public library exists to provide resources for everyone, perhaps most of all for those unable to buy books or computers for their own use. Children who do not 'learn to read' during the first three years of school experience enormous difficulty when they are subsequently asked to 'read to learn.' The disadvantage of not reading well is cataclysmic. Without the internalization of reading, there can be no information-seeking. The children's librarian may assist in this transformational process by helping the child articulate the answer to a question or concur with his or her observation and comment on what the book is about. In times past, children's librarians routinely listened to individual children speak about a book they had read in order to assess their comprehension of that book. Today, such listening can supplement the reference interview. Children's librarians can generate the highest profile of service within the community by interacting positively with children and parents through the reference interview. By bringing their children to the library, parents already acknowledge the role of the library and librarians in assisting the intellectual and prosocial behavior of their children. By being familiar with children and parents in their community, children's librarians can increase their effectiveness. By being familiar with young adults in their community, young adult librarians also increase their effectiveness. *A Fragile Foundation* (Benson et al., 1999: 40) has this to say regarding young people of today:

> Regardless of gender, cultural background, town size, or geographical location, today's young people typically: Receive too little support through sustained and positive intergenerational relationships; lack opportunities for leadership and involvement; disengage from youth-serving programs in the community; experience inconsistent or unarticulated boundaries; feel disconnected from and unvalued by their community; and miss the formation of social competencies and positive values.

Knowledge of these challenges can provide powerful service ideas. Claire K. Lipsman (1972) in *The Disadvantaged and Library Effectiveness* identified four recurring program elements that can be correlated with program effectiveness. These were:

1. competency and effectiveness of staff;
2. degree of community involvement and understanding of community dynamics;
3. degree of autonomy exercised by the project director in decision-making;
4. the quality of materials used; and
5. project visibility

Clearly, these elements should be kept in mind by youth services librarians contemplating successful programs. Each program's purpose should demonstrate a link to the mission statement of the public library.

Collection provision

It can be said that professional service to children in libraries begins with the collection and ends with the collection, but it really begins with the caregiver who takes the child to the library and creates for him or her an experience of the library. The reception the parent or caregiver is given by the library staff is often a significant factor in the use of the library and its programs. This welcoming attitude, encouraged by the mission statement and the library environment itself, can make all the difference in how the resources are used and enjoyed. This is one way to maximize access – another is to draw attention to the resources and staff available to support the entire family educationally. The nature of the audience determines the role of the youth services information specialist and how she or he makes information appropriately accessible to children and young adults. The Association for Library Service to Children (ALSC) states in its mission that the 'organization is committed to improving and ensuring the future of the nation.' This worthy goal is accomplished through 'exemplary library service to children, their families, and others who work with children' (*http://www.ala.org/ala/alsc/alsc.htm*).

Adolescents need to interact with peers and acquire a sense of belonging. They need to discuss conflicting values and formulate their own value systems along with acquiring their own identity in relationships with other people and ideas. Such activities as listening to music, watching television, reading popular magazines and books, and viewing movies, all contribute to peer interaction and provide adolescents with the opportunity for self-exploration. The librarian should try to recall the lived psychology of adolescence while choosing selections and give young adults the opportunity to be volunteers in storytelling. Resources which support the middle and high school curriculum are in demand in public libraries. Adolescents need the library as a quiet place in which to study, the Internet to help with homework, and a room for socializing and game playing. Visits to neighborhood middle and high schools to introduce the teen reading programs and deliver book talks on current young adult literature are effective marketing tools because the response can be measured in terms of circulation figures for the books featured (Bishop and Bauer, 2002). Press packs of pertinent information related to programming can be produced as handouts at the library and posted on the library web page. The pack could include a press release, which may feature a brief biographical sketch and photograph of the storyteller and directions and features of the teen online book club. Projects which might be used for programming can be solicited from the young adults in the library. The Young Adult Library Services Association (YALSA) website is an excellent source of projects to involve teens in strengthening their own networking mileu. In an article entitled 'Creativity, the name of the game in youth services,' Judy Haddad writes:

> The reference desk seems to have become a computer sign-up, DVD rental place of sorts, which is why libraries are now more than ever taking every opportunity to train school-aged children on an expansive use of the Internet and other online databases to help with their schoolwork. Many children simply know how to get on Yahooligans to play games or search Google to complete a report. It is up to the librarians to recommend appropriate sites for more extensive research and to promote proper techniques. But above all, we must stress to our young researchers that the Internet, while a wonderful tool, can be greatly complemented with a real book that one can hold and cherish. (Haddad, 2005: 6)

Selection

In the evaluation and selection of picture books, Carol Lynch-Brown and Carol Tomlinson (2005) noted criteria to help the librarian identify the best. Such criteria might also be applied to popular young adult novels: the elements of literature should be presented originally and racial, ethnic or sexual stereotyping in text and illustrations avoided. The language of the book needs to be rich, albeit not complicated, and interesting situations call for new vocabulary or vocabulary used in an original way.

Selecting picture books for storytime presentations takes time and experience and a willingness to experiment with what appeals to children. The book should be large enough so that a classroom of toddlers can see it. Learning concepts of literacy begin with holding a book correctly, turning the pages from left to right, distinguishing between print and illustration, and learning to identify the front of the book, the cover and the title. The storyteller can model these concepts for children. The picture books chosen for presentation should spark interest in the story and inspire a design to learn. The stories should be appropriate for the interests, ages and experience of the children and contain considerable action, strong beginnings, strong characters,

Reading is a family affair. Siblings learn a great deal from one another

(Photo by Jacek Chabraszewski. Courtesy Shutterstock 2007.)

and satisfactory endings. The text should be plainly and consistently placed on each page. The print should be large, and there should be adequate space between words to make them distinct. (This is particularly important when children begin to grasp the critical concept of one-to-one matching between the spoken word and the written word.)

An understanding of the preschool child's needs, cognitive abilities, psychosocial crises, and moral and social development can greatly enhance book selection. However, the librarian selecting literature for use with the preschool child should, if possible, pick materials that the adult likes personally. This intuitive liking for the selection is communicated to the child many times on different levels. The rationale for a positive personal experience of the literature on the librarian's part is that such an emotional reaction can more likely be drawn from the listeners; this is particularly important as the helper working with a preschool child will be engaged in reading the book aloud. It is also best if the librarian can select several similar books on a developmental theme, so the child has a voice in choosing the books with the greatest appeal. By using this strategy, a book is not forced upon a child with the implication that 'it's good for you.' There is a correct way to nurture literacy in the preschool child. As the librarian evaluates the child's response to any individual piece of literature, storytime selections can be refined until they are part of a professional storytime collection.

The librarian responsible for book selection in the circulating collection should be aware of the general aspects of selection for early childhood. Books should have:

- appealing illustrations, whether pictures or photographs, that enhance the text and make good use of color;

- interesting story content, which presupposes a logical development of events and portrays believable characters;
- useful information that is within the range of the child's understanding;
- broad humor, which needs to be fairly obvious for the preschool child;
- surprise elements, to create suspense and sustain interest;
- appealing, recurring refrains, which contribute familiarity and delight the child.

Deselection, or weeding, is the reverse side of selection. Automated circulation systems provide information about frequency of circulation, class of borrower, age of the item, language, and publisher. Circulation reports are useful tools for reordering and discarding, as they are based on the performance of the item, but as G. Edward Evans states:

> Although circulation data are as sound a predictor of future use as one can find, they rest upon several assumptions that staff must understand and accept. One assumption is that circulate use is proportional to in-house use. What that proportion is depends on local circumstances. Assumption two is that current use patterns are similar to past and future patterns. A third assumption is that statistically random samples provide an adequate base for determining use patterns. One known limitation of circulation data is that a few users can have a major impact on circulation (otherwise known as the 80/20 rule). Failure to take in-house use into account in a deselection program dependent on the use data as the main selection criterion will have skewed results. (Evans, 2005: 309)

The youth services librarian, in selecting all types of materials, evaluates the existing collection, determines what needs to be deselected, considers requests from parents and teachers, reads and selects from book reviews, and strives to balance subject area material provision to children for their homework reports and general interest reading needs. Picture books and beginning readers are very popular sections in the library needing constant enrichment. Evaluating one's own experience with how well the collection serves the needs of the public by circulation data and by observation of in-house use informs selection. Routinely, worn or lost materials which enjoyed strong circulation are replaced if they can be replaced. Web-based searches for out-of-print material often prove successful. A special line item budget for replacing such material can be made available for this purpose.

Reviewing sources

A few of the most well-known reviewing sources are listed here. Their web counterparts are easy to use and are preferable as reviewing sources because selections may be sent to vendors electronically. Purchasing is fully automated in most libraries. Although reading from a print reviewing source or viewing online are different experiences, the purpose of reading reviews is to provide a basis for selection which is grounded in the expertise of librarians and editors. Print copies of journals often provide the holistic experience of professional reading because they include articles. Brief annotations of some of the better known journals are given here:

- *The Bulletin of the Center for Children's Books* was founded in 1945 and reviews only current books for children. *The Bulletin* is one of the leading book review journals of children's books for school and public librarians in the United States. *The Bulletin* provides information on the content, reading level and quality of the books and makes suggestions for use in the curriculum.

- *No Flying, No Tights for Teens* (*http://www .noflyingnotights.com*) is a site dedicated to reviewing graphic novels for teens. Novels are grouped by genre. The site indicates which books are appropriate for younger teens. As graphic novels become more and more popular with patrons, this site keeps us up to date on the latest books. The site is easy to use and it is advantageous to have all the novels reviewed so the selection process can be faster and more accurate. Trends for teens change frequently and a site that can keep up is extremely valuable for the acquisition committee.

- *KLIATT* reviews young adult material. It is a bimonthly publication that is well organized. It offers a comprehensive table of contents at the beginning of each issue as well as an index in the back of all of the titles reviewed. The non-fiction review section is especially helpful because it is further divided into subjects. Many different subject areas are covered in the non-fiction section, which exposes the reader to more titles than they would normally encounter. *KLIATT* offers coding for age ranges, but the scope of the publication is young adult material, which makes this an ideal source for librarians only ordering such content.

- *Kirkus Reviews* contains three sections: Nonfiction, Fiction and Children's Books. Each review is listed alphabetically by the author's last name and the title of the book. The reviews are brief and include a description of the plot and other comments.

- *Booklist* is a monthly magazine published by the American Library Association and is the standard selection tool for libraries of all sizes. The reviews are organized by genre and age appeal. The magazine has occasional features such as 'Read-Alikes.' The magazine offers starred reviews and an annual Best of List, and contains short and concise reviews written by librarians on a wide variety of materials, including multimedia.

- *Bookmarks* compiles summaries of reviews from other major sources and magazines such as *Entertainment* and *Newsweek* to create guides to books. It is designed to be of interest to many types of readers and is arranged by theme.

- *VOYA – The Voice of Youth Advocates* is a bimonthly journal addressing librarians, educators, and other professionals who work with young adults. The only magazine devoted exclusively to the informational needs of teenagers, it was founded in 1978 by the librarians and renowned intellectual freedom advocates Dorothy M. Broderick and Mary K. Chelton 'to identify the social myths that keep us from serving young people and replace them with knowledge' (see *VOYA* website)

Working with budgets

At the state level, there are three major sources of funding available to public library systems in the US:

- local funds;
- state and federal funds; and
- tertiary funds.

Primary funding comes from ad valorem tax on taxable property within the municipality and/or the county. On average, local funding comprises approximately 70 percent of the of public library funding statement. State and federal funds in the form of grants are administered by state library commissions. Library officials are required to certify that they meet the requirements for program participation. Competitive LSTA grants are available to all public library systems and independent public libraries, consortia including a public library system, and associated organizations. The priorities, funding, and categories are subject to annual review by the state's Board of Commissioners. Capital improvement bond grants provide for new construction, repair and renovation, furniture and equipment, and technology. Tertiary funds, a third source of support for public libraries, are derived from fees and gifts. All funds, gifts, and memorials, once received on behalf of the library system, become public funds. The budget presentation is a request for continued and/or increased funding.

The board chair accompanies the public library director and assists with the budget request. A warrant or warrants constituting one-sixth of the annual appropriation for the support and maintenance of the library is given on a bi-monthly basis to the library director of each system. Accounting standards and procedures normally place the library administrative board of trustees in exclusive control of the finances of the library system and there is an obligation to uphold the public trust. To uphold this obligation of public trust with public funds, the library board should approve standards which the director and staff must adhere to concerning the business and financial operations of the system. The library budget depends on the appropriation allocated by the administrative board. The board approves and usually adopts the final form of the budget developed by the library director, and the library director, in turn, divides the operational budget into manageable parts.

Monies allocated to children's services are a subset of the actual operational budget for the library system; children and young adult library budgets address programming, collections or technology, or operating expenses. The budget request for children's and youth services resources and programs is therefore a planning document. Capital expenses such as buildings and staff salaries form the greatest proportion of the day-to-day operating expenses of the library. The library board approves standards which the director and staff must adhere to concerning the business and financial operation of the library system. Standards address the intent to comply with applicable laws, regulations and local practices, list the chain of command and the responsibilities of the parties involved, define standard operating procedures, ensure the retention of the required forms and records, and define the reporting and routing schedules.

Part 3

Professionalism

Library personnel

> The most important asset of any library goes home at night – the library staff. (Father Timothy Healy, Former President, New York Public Library)

Library personnel are the most important asset of the library because the library exists for the user. It can be said that professional service to children in libraries begins with the collection and ends with the collection, but without the caregiver who takes the child to the library there is no experience of the library. Without the service professional who welcomes the child and the caregiver, the experience of the library may not be as positive as it could be. The inculcation of a public service attitude in library staff is imperative, particularly for children and young adults. The Children's Services Vision Statement of the New Hamilton Public Library System is descriptive of the purpose of service:

> Our commitment is to provide an effective, efficient, accessible and specialized program of public library service to children, parents and caregivers of diverse interests and needs in order to promote library use and to create and nurture a lifelong interest in reading and learning. Service to children is a core service and is recognized as a key element in garnering and maintaining public support for library services. (Youth Services Report, 2002)

Molding youth into socially responsive working citizens begins in childhood and with parenting because children tend to model behavior, including that of the librarian. Personal enrichment of the child's family members is as important as it is for the child. In this way, the library supports an equalization process. Public libraries were created to serve those who do not have the means to buy their own resources. They were considered 'agents of culture' and places of access (Augst, 2001). Computers still provide access to exciting electronic information and software; however, part of the professionalism of the children's librarian is a sense of confidence in the timelessness of the role of information intermediary. The social characteristics of adolescents are related to their socialization needs and this occurs as they broaden their base of affiliation from family to peers. Opportunities for students to interact with peers and with adults in non-instructional areas of the library become more important at this age level.

Technology tends to be cumulative in its effect – interpreting the technology to the public is a way for the librarian to be an agent of change as well as culture. The reception the parent or caregiver is given by the librarian is a significant factor in the ease with which the collection is used. If the librarian is unhelpful to the parent or caregiver, the child or young adult may never want to return to the library. However, if the librarian takes time with a child or other patron and helps with book selection and location, the visitor is more likely to return and to make use of the various resources. In this way, the youth services professional cultivates a community of practice using the library resources and her commitment to service is a platform of cultivation. The 'helping process' of the youth services librarian is a highly professional attribute. According to W. Bernard Lukenbill 'The helping relationship concept itself is complex and diverse and involves a great deal of affective and/or empathetic behavior on the part of the helper in a professional role' (1977: 111). Lukenbill also cites D.D. Pettersen: 'The most important

Homework help in the library

(Photo by Jacek Chabraszewski. Shutterstock 2007.)

aspect of message communication is the relationship component of the message and not the message itself' (1977: 114). This relationship component should be the area in which youth services librarians excel. The professional role of nurturing human potential is taken up by teachers, doctors, psychologists, social workers, nurses, supervisors, counselors, human relations experts, psychiatrists, visiting teachers, personnel workers, guidance counselors, childcare specialists, and therapists. Such a role is also central to youth services librarianship. Suzanne Hildenbrand wrote that realistic library history has failed to show the centrality of women to library development and, by doing so, has made the collections of greater interest than the people who work in libraries (1996: 6). In many ways, the development of a deep and dynamic sense of social responsibility is necessary in the role of a youth services specialist. The deep-seated dynamics of such a sensibility are justice, respect, and love.

Because the librarian is able to facilitate access to the collection and may make the difference as to whether the collection is used or not, a welcoming attitude is the most effective way of removing the barriers between youth and information. There is probably no group in greater need than teenagers of the security a library's code of confidentiality offers. They can be educated to assume equal responsibility for confidentiality by safeguarding their library cards. A hallmark of professionalism is being aware of the impact staff may have on users of the library, particularly the impact of staff on young people. Another hallmark of professionalism is the integration of creative programming for children and young adults during holiday celebrations and school vacations. Census figures are important in planning services, as are library statistics on registration, circulation, and program attendance. The neighborhood newspaper and community directories, churches, community groups, and recreational facilities are other indicators of how the library can serve the populace well. Clearly, libraries (as well as schools) must be physically hospitable and inclusionary places for young people. Architecturally, children's rooms today are environmentally rich, mimicking cyberspace, and accommodate the imagination through computers, videos, and talking book software. Such tools emphasize the concept of exploration. Museums, playgrounds, and bookstores have served as models for multisensory and multimedia spaces (Kenney, 2006).

Library service and cultural diversity

Youth services librarians serve children and youth through collections, facilities, personnel, and programs. They pursue excellence and equity for all others and therefore respect diversity and multiculturalism. Multidimensional and multicultural print and electronic collections as well as sensitive staff are library resources which address cultural diversity and therefore literacy. Youth are also served through a network of local schools which contribute to democracy and community building within the city, state, and nation. One of the foundations of the profession is that everyone in the service community needs equal access to the information provided by libraries. Barriers to access can be physical or psychological. It makes sense that staff in libraries are themselves representatives of diversity as their presence promotes diversity in settings and resources. Rosemary du Mont et al. assert:

> The real measure of a library's commitment to diversity is most obvious at the point of contact with the patron. It is here that the degree of understanding of culturally diverse points of view and approaches become most significant. (1994: 10)

Pluralism is the new resource in designing library services, but is based on the old melting pot theory of homogeneity. Librarians can be change agents in their communities through incorporating solutions for the issues of diversity in society. Alire (1997) stated: 'We in Colorado can no longer ignore the fact that something needs to be done about meeting the information needs of the so-called have-nots.' She proposed the EthnicPops action plan for providing services to minority populations in public, academic, school, and special libraries in prisons and juvenile halls. This plan included a mentoring program for the retention and advancement of minority librarians. The heritage and culture of the local ethnic minority populations were promoted through cultural event programs such as celebrations. A Diversity Tool Kit which included important ethnic events, bookmarks, and a bibliography for library staff was made available through the state library. Such a partnership acknowledges that ethnic groups are treated with sensitivity, courtesy, and respect. Similarly, children from ethnic groups in the library community are to be treated with the sensitivity, courtesy and respect due them.

The provision of book collections for children in languages other than English is made based on the percentages of non-native speakers in the community. Budget allocations can be determined using these percentages. Including a wide selection of folktales from around the world addresses diversity in the library. The Mildred L. Batchelder Award is given to an American publisher for a children's book considered to be the most outstanding of those books originally published in a foreign language in a foreign country, and subsequently translated into English and published in the United States. The Association of Library Services to Children (ALSC) gives the award 'to encourage American publishers to seek out superior children's books abroad and to promote communication among the peoples of the world.' Batchelder spent 30 years with the ALA, working as an ambassador to the world on behalf of children and books, and encouraging and promoting the translation of the world's best children's literature. Her life's work was 'to eliminate barriers to understanding between people of different cultures, races, nations, and languages'. (See the Mildred L. Bachelder Award website.) Multiculturalism concerns are international, national, and local. Children have the right to services and materials that will provide for differences in cultural backgrounds and assist the child to reach his or her full potential as a human being.

Professional networking

At the World Library and Information Congress held in Oslo in 2005, Ivanka Stricevic, Chair of IFLA Libraries for Children and Young Adults Section, spoke of how the activities of the section:

> ... are related to the promotion and encouragement of all types of literacies for all children and young adults especially of the skills required by the new technological age, and to the development of partnership for the enrichment and exchange of resources. (Stricevic, 2005)

International advocacy of this type indicates a global recognition of the professionalism of children's librarianship. In 2004, Kathy East reported on the *Promotion of the Children's Guidelines* at the World Library and Information Congress held in Buenos Aires, Argentina, noting that in 1991 Adele Fasick stated in the original *Guidelines for Children's Services* that the overarching goal of children's library work was 'to offer to children access to the knowledge and culture of the society in which he or she is growing up.' At home in every society, children's librarianship as a profession is interpreted through the librarian's relationship with the parent and caregiver network which brings the children to the library. The culture of family generates the engagement of the children with the library, just as family culture assists in identity formation. As mentioned previously, family literacy programming such as story time and popular author engagements define the public library for children as a context within which literacy strategies are developed and the public self can emerge. The emergence of the public self in adolescence is similarly a developmental task.

The interpretation of the patron's information needs by children's librarians may be seen in terms of the child's social milieu and of the relationships shared with the significant others in his or her life. Children assist each other and communicate with those closest around them in interpreting the resources of the library. Siblings tend to form a social network which can be effectively utilized for information provision on the part of the children's librarian. This social network carries the key to lifelong learning. The connection between library use and good parenting can be seen in how parents help children become prosocial. Asking the children questions regarding their information needs clarifies their own ideas of what the library holds for them. Learning theories that are based on the personal and social interactions of adults and children and children using books with other children are foremost in significance for literacy development because children instinctively place their ideas within that network. The children's librarian, by knowing the parents, teachers, and children in the community, and by emphasizing the role of the family through programming and collections, encourages literacy development. By knowing the young adult community, the youth services librarian can cater to the information needs of the young adults themselves.

Encountering censorship

Librarians are charged to act as evaluators (as opposed to censors) when they acquire materials, and to apply normative criteria as they compare materials and choose to include items. The issue of selection versus censorship as interpreted in the acquisitions policy is of fundamental concern to the profession and an example of the opposition between collective rights and individual rights. No genre of information is exempt from censorship, whether scientific, fiction or propaganda. Jenkinson (1986) wrote that the censor as a human agent acting in the social process might do any of the following: look for items to exclude from the collection, search for what might be discarded, judge a book on the basis of a few disliked passages, rely on the reviews of other censors to eliminate books, want the collection to include only books that represent a preferred point of view, or look outside the book for reasons to reject it (for example, the author's religion or politics). John Stuart Mill believed that unfettered discussion was the best way to promote truth, and that all ideas, even the most offensive, preposterous or potentially injurious, can be expressed and should be allowed. He believed that truth would always triumph over falsehood provided that there were no restrictions on expression (Doyle, 1998). Nevertheless, demeaning images are unacceptable in public library collections. Because the Internet combines characteristics of the newspaper, telephone, radio, television, and computer, the opportunities for wrongdoing in cyberspace are complex. On the other hand, opportunities for beneficial endeavors such as those promoting education, research, commerce, entertainment, and discourse on public affairs is crucial in a pluralistic world. Knowledge of the tension apparent in collection provision, particularly for young adults (because of the controversial content of many young adult novels), will assist librarians in valuing the collection development policy as a document of communication and diplomacy within and without the library.

The author's daughter uses the computer at the Petal Public Library, MS

(Photo by Susan Higgins, 2007.)

Role of the youth services manager

The traditional role of the information specialist as one who selects, organizes, and facilitates easy access to information changes somewhat in the arena of youth service. Although the youth service librarian clearly does do this, it is done through the development and implementation of programmes. The youth service manager will maintain the department's budget by controlling the amount spent, make records of the department's monthly statistics and reports, make presentations to school and civic groups, and perform other duties as identified by the director of the library. The benefits of such employment are a retirement system, paid holidays, the accumulation of vacation and sick leave, and the opportunity to be part of a growing and multifaceted profession. At the entry-level, a bachelor's degree in library science or a closely related field is required. A master's degree in library and information science will command a higher entry-level salary and promotional opportunity unavailable at the entry-level salary scale. The seven areas of competency for work with youth according to the Association for Library Service to Children (ALSC) are:

- knowledge of the client group;
- administrative and managerial skills;
- communications skills;
- materials and collection development;
- programming skills;
- advocacy;
- public relations and networking; and
- professionalism and professional development.

Denise Adkins analysed youth services job advertisements using the methodology of content analysis. Her findings indicated:

> The number of advertised youth services positions is increasing, and job titles are changing from the specific 'children's services' to the more generalized 'youth services.' Advertised responsibilities of the youth services librarian have consistently emphasized collection management and administrative duties, and

many advertisements place a heavy emphasis on personality traits. (2004: 59).

The Master of Library Science (MLS) degree, working experience, and knowledge of children's literature were job requirements mentioned in the advertisements, while targeted personality traits were energy, enthusiasm and creativity (Adkins, 2004: 67).

The primary thrust for future youth service professionals will continue to be centered on the contextual, managerial, technological, and service aspects of their jobs. In practising such competencies, each team member of the youth services support team needs to understand and communicate the vision, mission, and priorities of the library in order to move the collection toward its goals. Team members need to be committed to excellent service, process improvement, and continuous learning. This includes participation in the planning and decision-making processes of customer services, obtaining the information necessary to perform the job, accepting change, and being willing to participate in library-wide issues and concerns. Within the library, maintaining a customer service orientation to one another is ideal. Such an orientation challenges oneself and colleagues to think creatively. Prioritizing work and assisting others on the team by becoming involved with cross-functional projects demonstrates flexibility. Creating community-wide partnerships to develop grant applications for national organizations broadens the vision of the youth services librarian. It is within such parameters of leadership that ideas can flourish. The ability to communicate with senior management using a business approach which describes the value of information services to youth is also a critical component of competency. Qualitative findings describing thematic approaches to the users' voiced concerns are important. They are important because some of the findings of the latest National Center for Education Statistics survey on Services and Resource for Children and Young Adults in Public Libraries were that 60 per cent of the 18 million people entering public libraries during a typical week were youth, and only one youth specialist was available for every 618 youths. The percentage of libraries with children's and young adult librarians has not changed since the late 1980s. The ethnic diversity of children and young adult patrons has increased by 40 percent in US public libraries over the last five years. Librarians report that insufficient library staff is a major barrier to increasing services and resources for youth (US Center for Education Statistics).

Such statistics bring to light the importance of services as well as the principles of services to the underserved. The library needs of children and young adults must be understood and acknowledged in all policy- and decision-making areas, including the work of non-public departments. Children should have equality of opportunity with all other client groups as far as access to library provision and services is concerned. Detailed knowledge of children's development, children's literature, IT software and networks, and educational matters necessarily implies a specialist element within the staffing structure. An appropriate recruitment and selection policy should exist whereby the library needs of children are recognized in all public library and school library job descriptions and employee specifications. Positive measures should be taken to recruit staff who reflect the makeup of the community. The American Library Association, through various grants and scholarship initiatives, seeks to encourage students of color to pursue higher education. Mentorship programs are important tools of accommodation.

Marketing and promotional activities

In *Selection and Design of Services*, Mae Benne (1991) suggested that children's services can be broken down into basic services and programming. Basic services are ongoing and available on an individual basis while programming involves activities selected to support specific objectives and are offered to groups, either occasionally or regularly. Examples of basic services would be the reference or information services as well as material selection. Benne notes that librarians who serve children and young adults often allocate more of their resources to programming than their counterparts in the adult services department. Programs are designed to be enjoyable learning experiences for children and are compatible with the learning objectives of teachers. Programs are high-profile services which are intended to be flexibly scheduled and visible in the community. Basic services and programming are marketable services.

The fundamentals of programming are:

1. Review the library's mission statement for direction.
2. Determine the priority level assigned this objective.
3. Have procedures in place for enlisting suggestions from staff and outside personnel as needed.
4. Determine what actions, if any, should be taken by others before and during planning.
5. Devise a timetable for action. (Benne, 1991: 69)

It is also important to design an evaluation for the programme, so that comments can be incorporated into an improved delivery when the program is repeated or redesigned. Attendance figures are always recorded for the library's annual report.

Early Literacy Events for children can be promoted by the mayor's council and bring community acknowledgement for the importance of reading and writing. Such events may take place in the city park and feature special readings of children's books by officials. If a university is located in the area, collaboration with the Department of Education is possible. Project SEED is funded by the US Department of Health and Human Services, while Administration on Children and Families may also provide funding.

According to Peggy Johnson (2004), library websites that list and point to related sources have superseded the preparation of bibliographic material in libraries. That the website is attractive and current and serves the purpose of an informational electronic bulletin board of programs and services available at the library is common sense. However, regular face-to-face contact with users increases the odds of a responsive collection, the basic marketing tool of professionalism.

Conceptually, marketing consists of finding out what the user needs and how, where, and when it can best be delivered, and sometimes what the user is willing to pay. As Dresang et al. state: 'The first goal of marketing research is user satisfaction and recognition of the opportunities to respond to user needs in ways that make sense in terms of the library's strategic plan' (2006: 70).

Evaluation of programs and services

For many years, librarians have used surveys, focus groups, interviews, and observation to measure user satisfaction with public library services and programs. Durrance and Fisher (2003) wrote that accountability to codify outcomes in library service reaches a high-water mark in professional librarianship. Satisfaction with services is often held up to the mission statement as an indicator of priorities and subsequent resource allocation. Today, evaluation of youth services programs is strongly linked to program results or outcomes which in turn provide justification for planning as well as accountability in government agencies and other non-profit organizations for funds allocation.

Dresang et al. (2006) advocate the use of an outcome-based planning and evaluation (OBPE) model to assist in accumulating meaningful data on programs for children and young adults. This model was developed with the support of an Institute of Museum and Library Services national leadership grant and library and information science researchers at Florida State University. As Virginia Walter explains in her foreword, the CATE (Children's Access to and Use of Technology Evaluation) OBPE model asks librarians to 'start with desired outcomes based on market research and community analysis, then work backward and design the service or program that will achieve the outcome in question and design an evaluation strategy to see if we meet the target' (Walter, 2006: foreword). The title of the program, a description of the program, and a desired outcome type are mapped in table form. The authors suggest three levels of design: 'Level I, a single program, offered once or repeated; Level II, a group of programs on a common topic or theme; or Level III, a multifaceted program' (Dresang et al., 2006: 41). Desired outcomes such as 'Children obtain a library card to encourage them to become regular library users' or 'Young children gain respect for forest environments' are communicated to all participants so that the interests and needs of various age groups and methods of stimulating reading, listening or gaining technological skills are emphasized. For young adult programs, it is suggested that program outcomes are developed with the input of young adults (so that they are given the power of decision-making and therefore the exercise of intellectual freedom).

Because SWOT (Strengths, Weaknesses, Opportunities and Threats) analysis has been used by youth services teams as a method to brainstorm guidelines, services, and programs, the platform can be used for follow-up work with the OBPE forms to create a planning document. It is easy to see that the marketing and evaluation of programs and services are interrelated concepts because young services specialists are constantly marketing and evaluating the success of programs. Surveys can be a management tool. Based in the Department of Library and Information Services at Loughborough University in the UK, LISU (the Library and Information Statistics Unit) is an internationally renowned research and information center for library and information services. LISU collects, analyses, interprets, and publishes statistical information for and about the library domain in the United Kingdom on behalf of the Museums, Archives and Libraries Council. All aspects of survey design, processing, and analysis are addressed: the development and interpretation of management statistics, tailored seminars and workshops, statistical benchmarking, performance evaluation and improvement, and evidence-based management support for quantitative and qualitative methods/approaches. Each year, LISU publishes an extensive annual report on the provision and use of public library services to schools and children. The series can be useful as a management tool for both public and school library services, allowing comparison and benchmarking against other authorities and the wider national picture.

Networking in the community for jointly sponsored events

Networking services in the community rests on an awareness of existing opportunities for youth in the community and plans to deepen staff knowledge of buildings and collections and strengthen liaisons with staff at other libraries. Networking is about resource sharing – both of materials and staff expertise for the mutual benefit of children and young adults in the community. The presence of a special collection of children's literature, sometimes housed in the local university, presents a networking opportunity for neighboring public libraries and school libraries, even if only in the form of a guided tour. Museums and libraries share a common educational role and events including children from public libraries and school libraries enjoy informational programming. Children's museums in the community are designed especially for a hands-on experience. Young Authors' Conferences affiliated with local elementary schools are another way of advertising what literature collections in public libraries hold for children. Networking as a professional tool is the essence of public relations and marketing because, by offering programmes outside the library, children and their parents will be more interested in finding out what is occurring inside the library (Pfiel, 2005). Networking can enlarge the audience of children served, and ultimately expand available library services and programming throughout regional or city library systems. State library consultants for public libraries can provide consultation on the development, improvement and extension of library operations and services to public libraries regionally and locally. Bookbags, posters, etc. serve as marketing materials for summer reading programs. Youth services librarians visit schools to introduce the summer reading programs prior to the end-of-year ceremonies.

Networking on behalf of young adults

The lack of assurance that typically marks adolescence can be characterized by overreaction or withdrawal from social contact. Use of the Internet as a primary information and recreational resource may make it appear that young adults are totally independent of social learning needs. The presence of a mature youth services librarian who has channeled and controlled human traits such as shyness within herself/himself can balance the young adult's personality. This willingness to be the 'balancing act' is an aspect of leadership. The resources and programming specialized for this audience may be accepted and used primarily because of the effect the specialist has. A significantly positive difference can be made in satisfaction by welcoming the young adults to the library, in their use of interlibrary loan, their knowledge of hotline information, their use of programming and activities, their interest in the popular materials collection, their enjoyment of related booklists on young adult reading, and the provision of an area for playing games (Higgins, 1992).

The Search Institute, an independent non-profit organization, seeks to provide leadership, knowledge and resources to promote healthy youth and communities. Peter L. Benson, President and CEO of the Institute, has introduced forty 'developmental assets' or building blocks of healthy development:

> These assets – such as family support, intergener-
> ational relationships, clear and consistent boundaries
> and expectations, participation in constructive
> activities, and community focus on values – are
> essential for all youth, regardless of background. Yet
> too few young people have these support structures in
> their lives. (Search Institute website)

The Institute provides funding every year for selected public
libraries to implement youth services programming which
addresses one or more of the developmental assets outlined
by the Institute. Patrick Jones spoke of the organization as
responsible for recovering his passion for public libraries:

> The key research finding is this: the more assets young
> people have, the more likely they are to thrive as teens,
> then become caring competent adults that contribute
> to society rather than take from it. No, the assets are
> not the holy grail of solving every youth problem, but
> the strength based asset approach is research
> grounded, easy to understand and sell, and all the
> evidence suggest this: it works. (Jones, in Horrocks,
> 2005: 75)

Research topics

Doctoral research into public library service to youth tends
to revolve around children and young adults as users with
special needs and the provision of specialized staff and
resources to meet these needs. How these needs are met
presently and how they were met historically is of continual
interest. Comparative studies of youth librarianship
internationally are welcome, as services to children globally

encompass the library as 'providing a cultural space to have fun, read and to think' (Young, 2006). Other areas which are in need of research attention were addressed in a literature review presented by Melissa Gross at the ALISE (Association for Library and Information Science Education) meeting in San Antonio in January 2006. These include the codification of best practice and the evaluation of youth services in libraries, including outcomes, policy research, the relationship between the public library and other organizations, and the children's room as a specialized space in the library. Studies addressing how children interact with digital resources, including digital reference services, are also needed as well as comparisons of child and adult use of such resources. Mary K. Chelton (2004) asks for an explanation of the place of electronic resources within other resources for youth since children and young adults make extensive use of technology and digital imaging. More research is needed on instant messaging, e-mail communication, chat rooms, and blogs. Christine Jenkins (2001) and Virginia Walter (2001) write extensively on the history of youth services in the pubic library and provide historical research into youth literature as well as comparative studies of youth librarianship. Jenkins (2006) also examines critical standards for youth literature, book publishing, and popular culture and oral histories (see: *http://people.lis.uiuc.edu/ncajenkin/research.html*).

Children and young adults themselves need to be involved in research (Gross, 2006). Students can often find ideas for research in the recommendations for further study sections of doctoral dissertations which frequently address many aspects of youth services and public libraries. Schools of library and information science themselves often provide opportunities for alumni to consult with current students, maintain contact with classmates and develop and recognize distinguished achievement within the university family.

For the practitioner, dissemination of research results and the application of results to practice will assist in interpreting services in a new light and provide justification for the 'why' of services. In this way, research in the field can add value to the practice of librarianship.

Conclusion

For most of the twentieth century, religious organizations, social service agencies, and social clubs have been engaged in providing educational, recreational, and vocational services for youth around the globe. Linda Alexander and Barbara Immroth comment:

> Youth services in public libraries have grown and adapted for more than a century, as youth librarians have worked with commitment and focus to define and develop services appropriate for young people. (2004: 211)

Today the inclusion of positive development as a purpose of library services to youth addresses both relationships with parents and community needs for engagement as well as strategies for countering the underlying causes of problem behaviors. Youth services librarians are interested in creating positive outcomes for youth such as competence and confidence. These outcomes enhance the quality of life for the individual, the organization and the world. Alexander and Immroth (2004) wrote that relationships with adults can affect the child's or young adult's entire school career. Through the experience of connection with the community by means of the relationship with the librarian, youth can not only find themselves and their place in the world, but can make an important connection and contribution to their own lives and those of others.

References

Adkins, D. (2004) 'Changes in public library youth services: a content analysis of youth services job advertisements,' *Public Library Quarterly*, 23 (3/4): 59–73.

Adkins, D. and Higgins, S.E. (2006) 'Education for library service to youth in five countries,' *New Review of Children's Literature and Librarianship*, 12 (1): 33–48.

Agosto, D.E. (2006) *Criteria for Evaluating Multicultural Literature*. Available at: *http://www.pages.drexel.edu/~dea22/multicultural.html* (accessed 7 July 2006).

Agosto, D.E. and Hughes-Hassell, S. (2006) 'Toward a model of everyday life information needs of urban teenagers, part 1: theoretical model,' *Journal of the American Society for Information Science and Technology*, 57 (10): 1394–403.

Albanese, A.R. (2006) 'The social life of books: conversation with Ben Vershbow,' *Library Journal*, 131 (9): 28–30.

Alexander, L.B. and Immroth, B. (2004) 'Youth services in public libraries', in K. McCook (ed.), *Introduction to Public Librarianship*. New York: Neal-Schuman.

Alire, C.A. (1997) 'Ethnic populations: a model for statewide service,' *American Libraries*, 28 (10): 38–40.

Americans with Disabilities Act 1990 – see: *http://www.eeoc.gov/abouteeoc/35th/1990s/ada.html* (accessed 18 January 2007).

Arrighetti, J. (2001) 'The challenge of unattended children

in the public library,' *Reference Services Review*, 29 (1): 65–71.

Augst, T. (2001) 'Introduction: libraries as agencies of culture,' *American Studies*, 42 (3): 5–22.

Baker, S.L. and Lancaster, W. (1991) *The Measurement and Evaluation of Library Services*, 2nd edn. Arlington, VA: Information Resources Press.

Belanger, J. (2002) 'Selling and promoting to libraries: what are publishers and vendors doing to reach libraries?' in H. Edelman and R.P. Holley (eds), *Marketing to Libraries for the New Millennium: Librarians, Vendors and Publishers Review the Landmark Third Industry-Wide Survey of Library Marketing Practices and Trends*. Lanham, MD: Scarecrow Press.

Benne, M. (1991) *Principles of Children's Services in Public Libraries*. Chicago, IL: American Library Association.

Benson, P.L., Scales, P.C., Leffert, N., and Roehlkepartain, E.C. (1999) *Fragile Foundation: The State of Developmental Assets Among American Youth*. Chicago: Independent Publisher's Group.

Bernhardt, E.B. (1991) *Reading Development in a Second Language*. Norwood, NJ: Ablex.

Berry, J.N. (2006) 'Everyone's hitching post,' *Library Journal*, 131 (2): 38–41.

Bishop, K. and Bauer, P. (2002) 'Attracting young adults to public libraries: Frances Henne/YALSA/VOYA Research Grant results,' *JOYS*, Winter: 36–43.

Bishop, K. and Salveggi, A. (2001) 'Responding to developmental stages in reference service to children,' *Public Libraries*, November/December: 354–8.

Blanshard, C. (1998) *Managing Library Services for Children and Young People: A Practical Handbook*. London: Library Association Publishing.

Bontempo, B.T. (1995) 'Exploring prejudice in young adult

literature through drama and role play,' *The Alan Review*, 22 (3). Available at: *http://scholar.lib.vt.edu/ejournals/ALAN/spring95/Bontempo.html* (accessed 29 November 2006).

Braverman, M. (1979) *Youth, Society, and the Public Library*. Chicago: American Library Association.

Brazleton, T.B. (1992) *Touchpoints: Your Child's Emotional and Behavioral Development*. Reading, MA: Addison-Wesley.

Broderick, D.M. (1977) *Library Work with Children*. New York: H.W. Wilson.

Carlson, A.D. (1991) *The Preschooler and the Library*. Metuchen, NJ: Scarecrow Press.

Carlson Weeks, A. (1987) *Current Trends in Public Library Service for Children*. Champaign, IL: University of Illinois, Graduate School of Library and Information Science.

Chelton, M.K. (1983) 'Young adult reference services in the public library,' *Reference Librarian*, 7/8: 31–45.

Chelton, M.K. (1989) 'The first national survey of services and resources for young adults in public libraries', *Journal of Youth Services in Libraries*, 2: 224–31.

Chelton, M.K. and Cool, C. (2004) *Youth Information Seeking Behavior: Theories, Models, and Issues*. Lanham, MD: Scarecrow Press.

Chowdhury, G., Poulter, A., and McMenemy, D. (2006) 'Public Library 2.0: towards a new mission for public libraries as a "networked of community knowledge,"' *Online Information Review*, 30 (4): 454–60.

Cohen, R. (2006) 'YALSA Research Committee selects 2006 Frances Henne YALSA/VOYA (Voice of Youth Advocates) Research Grant recipient.' See: *http://www.ala.org/ala/yalsa/newsandeventsb/henne.htm* (accessed 18 January 2007).

Combes, B. (2006) 'Techno savvy or techno oriented: who

are the net generation?' in *Proceedings of the Asia-Pacific Conference on Library and Information Education and Practice: Preparing Information Professionals for Leadership in the New Age*, Singapore, 3–6 April, pp. 401–8.

Crew, H.S. (1997) 'Feminist scholarship and theories of adolescent development: implications for young adult services in libraries,' *Journal of Youth Services in Libraries*, 10: 405–17.

Curry, A. (2005) 'If I ask, will they answer? Evaluating public library reference service to gay and lesbian youth,' *Reference and User Services Quarterly*, 45 (1): 65–75.

Daniel, M.C. (2005) 'Helping linguistic minorities read independently,' *Academic Exchange Quarterly*, 9 (2).

Delors, J. (1996) 'Education: the necessary utopia,' in *Learning: The Treasure Within*, Report to UNESCO of the International Commission on Education for the Twenty-First Century. Unesco Publishing.

Denham, D. and Elkin, J. (1997) 'A place for children: the qualitative impact of public libraries on children's reading: interim report,' *New Review of Children's Literature and Librarianship*, 3: 93–103.

Donaldson, M. (1979) *Children's Minds*. New York: Norton.

Douglass College (2000) *Evaluating Electronic Information Resources for Young Women: General Research Concepts*, Douglass Project for Rutgers Women in Math, Science, and Engineering and the Girl Scouts of the USA. See: *http://girlstech.douglass.rutgers.edu/PDF/completereport.pdf* (accessed 1 March 2007).

Downey, T.W. (1979) 'YA services: 1993,' *Top of the News*, 35: 347–53.

Doyle, T. (1998) 'A Millian critique of library censorship,' *Journal of Academic Librarianship*, 24 (3): 241–3.

Dresang, E.T., Gross, M., and Holt, L.E. (2006) *Dynamic*

Youth Services through Outcome-Based Planning and Evaluation. Chicago: American Library Association.

Du Mont, R.R., Butler, L., and Caynon, W. (1994) *Multiculturalism in Libraries.* Westport, CT: Greenwood Press.

Dungworth, N., Grimshaw, S., McKnight, C., and Morris, A. (2004) 'Reading for pleasure? A summary of the findings from a survey of the reading habits of year 5 pupils,' *New Review of Children's Literature and Librarianship,* 10 (2): 169–88.

Durrance, J.C. and Fisher, K.E. (2003) 'Determining how libraries and librarians help,' *Library Trends,* 51 (4): 305–34.

East, K. (2004) *Promotion of Children's Guidelines: Introducing the Guidelines for Children's Libraries Services: The Presentation of the First English Edition and the Spanish Translation.* World Library and Information Congress, 70th IFLA General Conference and Council, 22–27 August 2004, Buenos Aires, Argentina. See: *http://www.ifla.org/IV/ifla69/prog03.htm* (accessed 19 January 2007)..

Edelman, H. and Holley, R.P. (2002) *Marketing to Libraries for the New Millennium: Librarians, Vendors, and Publishers Review the Landmark Third Industry-wide Survey of Library Marketing Practices and Trends.* Lanham, MD: Scarecrow Press.

Edmonds, L. (1989) *Managers and Missionaries: Library Services to Children and Young Adults in the Information Age,* Allerton Park Institute Proceedings No. 28. Urbana-Champaign, IL: University of Illinois, Graduate School of Library and Information Science.

Edwards, M. (1969) *The Fair Garden and the Swarm of Beasts.* New York: Hawthorn Books.

Evans, G. Edward (2005) *Developing Library and*

Information Center Collections, 5th edn. Westport, CT: Libraries Unlimited.

Everhart, N. and Valenza, J. (2004) 'Research into practice: Internet-savvy students and their schools,' *Knowledge Quest*, 32 (4): 50–5.

Fasick, A.M. (1984) 'Moving into the future without losing the past: children's services in the information age,' *Library Trends*, 40 (4): 405–13.

Fasick, A.M. (1991) *Guidelines for Children's Services*, Section of Children's Libraries. Supplement to *Guidelines for Public Libraries* (1986), IFLA Professional Report No. 25. IFLA.

Fasick, A.M. (1998) *Managing Children's Services in the Public Library*, 2nd edn. Englewood, CO: Libraries Unlimited.

Fasick, A.M. and England, C. (1977) *Children Using Media: Reading and Viewing – Preferences among the Users and Non-Users of the Regina Public Library. Research Report.* Toronto: Centre for Research in Librarianship, Faculty of Library Science, University of Toronto.

Feinberg, S., Kuchner, J.F., and Feldman, S. (1998) *Learning Environments for Young Children: Rethinking Library Spaces and Services.* Chicago: American Library Association.

Fiore, C. (2005) *Fiore's Summer Reading Program Handbook.* New York: Neal-Schuman.

Fisher, D.C. (1929) 'Children's librarians,' in Committee on Library Work with Children of the American Library Association, *Children's Library Yearbook No. 1.* Chicago: American Library Association.

Fisher, H. (2000) 'Children's librarians: where are they?' *Orana*, March: 9–13.

Fletcher, W.I. (1876) 'Public libraries and the young,' in *Public Libraries in the United States: Their History,*

Condition and Management. Washington, DC: Department of the Interior, Bureau of Education.

Flum, J.G. (1983) 'The young adult and personal crisis information needs: how can libraries help?' *Catholic Library World*, 54 (7): 275–7.

Foreman, J. (2003) 'Next-generation: educational technology versus the lecture,' *EDUCAUSEreview*, July/August: 12–22.

Fox, M. (1992) 'Lessons from a home,' in A. Kwan-Terry and P. Bodycott (eds), *Reading and Writing in a Multicultural Society*. Singapore: Society for Reading and Literacy.

Georgia Public Library Services (n.d.) 'Children's services.' Available at: *http://www.georgialibraries.org/lib/child.html* (accessed 7 July 2006).

Gorman, M. (2004) *Library Values in a Changing World*. Keynote address to the Canadian Library Association, CLA/BCLA Resource Centre, 17 June, Victoria, British Columbia. See: *http://www.cla.ca/resources/cla_bcla2004/index.htm* (accessed 17 January 2007).

Grams, A. (1969) 'Understanding the adolescent reader,' *Library Trends*, 17: 121–31.

Greiner, J. M. (1994) 'Research issues in public librarianship: a bibliographic essay', in J.M. Greiner (ed.), *Research Issues in Public Librarianship: Trends for the Future*. Westport, CT: Greenwood Press.

Gross, M. (2006) *Listening to Ourselves: Developing an Action Plan for Youth Services*. Available at: *http://www.uky.edu/smcqu2/alise/youth_services/confer/2006alise/Gross_Listening.pdf* (accessed 22 June 2006).

Gunn, B.K., Simmons, D.C., and Kameenui, E.J. (2006) *Emergent Literacy: Synthesis of the Research*. See: *http://idea.uoregon.edu/~ncite/documents/techrep/tech19.html* (accessed 18 January 2007).

Haddad, J. (2005) 'Creativity, the name of the game in youth services,' *Illinois Library Association Report*, 23 (1): 6–8.

Hannigan, J.A. (1994) 'A feminist standpoint for library and information science education,' *Journal of Education for Library and Information Science*, 35 (4): 297–319.

Harris, M. (2005) 'Contemporary ghost stories: cyberspace in fiction for children and young adults', *Children's Literature in Education*, 36 (2): 111–28.

Healy, Father Timothy (Former President, New York Public Library) (n.d.) 'Quotes about Librarians, Libraries, Books, and Reading.' Available at: *http://www. statelibraryofiowa.org/ld/tell-library-story/scpt/quotes-about-libraries* (accessed 3 May 2006).

Hearne, B. (1996) 'Margaret K. McElderry and the professional matriarchy of children's books,' *Library Trends*, 44 (4): 755–75.

Higgins, S. (1992) *A Study of the Effectiveness of Public Library Service to Young Adults.* Doctoral dissertation, Florida State University.

Higgins, S.E. (2000/1) 'Information, technology and diversity: censorship in the 21st century,' in G.E. Gorman (ed.), *International Yearbook of Library and Information Management 2000/2001: Collection Management.* London: Library Association.

Higgins, S.E. (2001/2) 'Youth services in an electronic environment,' in G.E. Gorman (ed.), *International Yearbook of Library and Information Management 2001/2002: Information Services in an Electronic Environment.* London: Library Association.

Higgins, S. and Hawamdeh, S. (2001) 'Gender and cultural aspects of information seeking and use,' *New Review of Information Behavior Research: Studies of Information Seeking in Context*, 2 (Spring): 17–28.

Hildenbrand, S. (1996) *Reclaiming the American Library Past: Writing the Women In*. Norwood, NJ: Ablex.

Hill, R.A. (2006) *The Secret Origin of Good Readers: A Resource Book*. Christopher Higginson and SLG Publishing. Available at: *http://www.night-flight.com/secretorigin/index.html* (accessed 20 July 2006).

Hilyard, N.B. (2002) 'Assets and outcomes: new directions in young adult services in public libraries,' *Public Libraries*, 41 (4): 195–9.

Hine, L.W. (n.d.) *Child Labor in America, 1908–1912: Photographs of Lewis W. Hine*. Available at: *http://www.historyplace.com/unitedstates/childlabor/about.htm* (accessed 21 July 2006).

Hinton, S.E. (2003) *The Outsiders*. New York: Speak/Penguin Putnam.

Horning, K.T. (1994) 'How can I help you? The joys and challenges of reference work with children,' *Show-Me Libraries*, 45: 9–19.

Horrocks, N. (2005) *Perspectives, Insights and Priorities: 17 Leaders Speak Freely of Librarianship*. Lanham, MD: Scarecrow Press.

Howard, V. (2006) 'Teens and pleasure reading: a critical assessment from Nova Scotia,' in M.K. Chelton and C. Cool (eds), *Youth Information-Seeking Behavior: Theories, Models and Issues*, Vol. 2. Lanham, MD: Scarecrow Press. Available at: *http://www.cais-acsi.ca/proceedings/2006/howard_2006.pdf* (accessed 9 July 2006).

Hughes-Hassell, S. and Mancall, J.C. (2005) *Collection Management for Youth: Responding to the Needs of Learners*. Chicago: American Library Association.

Hurst, C. (2006) 'Children's literature site.' Available at: *http://users.crocker.com/~rebotis/* (accessed 6 June 2006).

Husband, R. and Foster, W. (1987) 'Understanding

qualitative research: a strategic approach to qualitative methodology,' *Journal of Humanistic Education and Development*, 26 (2): 50–63.

Immroth, B. (1989) 'Improving children's services: competencies for librarians serving children in public libraries,' *Public Libraries*, May–June: 166–74.

Jay, H.L. and Jay, M.E. (1984) *Developing Library–Museum Partnerships to Serve Young People*. Hamden, CT: Library Professional Publications.

Jenkins, C. (2001a) 'The history of youth services librarianship: a review of the research literature', *Libraries and Culture*, 35: 103–40.

Jenkins, C. (2001b) 'International harmony: threat or menace? US youth services librarians and Cold War censorship, 1946–1955,' *Libraries and Culture*, 36 (1): 116–30.

Jenkins, C. (2006) *Research Statement*. See: *http://people .lis.uiuc.edu/~cajenkin/research.html* (accessed 19 January 2007).

Jenkinson, E.B. (1986) *The Schoolbook Protest Movement: 40 Questions and Answers*. Bloomington, IN: Phi Delta Kappa Educational Foundation.

Jerome Bruner and the Process of Education (n.d.) Available at: *http://www.infed.org/thinkers/bruner.htm* (accessed 11 August 2005).

Johnson, P. (2004) *Fundamentals of Collection Development and Management*. Chicago: American Library Association.

Jones, P. (2002) *New Directions for Library Service to Young Adults*. Chicago: American Library Association.

Jones, P. (2005) 'Meet the new boss, same as the old boss: a personal view of librarianship', in N. Horrocks (ed.), *Perspectives, Insights and Priorities: 17 Leaders Speak Freely of Librarianship*. Oxford: Scarecrow Press.

Jones, P., Gorman, M., and Suellentrop, T. (2004) *Connecting Young Adults and Libraries: A How-To-Do-It Manual for Librarians*, 3rd edn. Portland, OR: Book News.

Keller, H. (1905) *The Story of My Life*, Chapter 1. See: *http://www.worldwideschool.org/library/books/hst/biogr aphy/StoryofMyLife/chap7.html* (accessed 19 January 2007).

Kenney, B. (2006) Welcome to the fun house: when is a children's room not a children's room? When it's the trove,' *Library Journal*, Spring Supplement.

KidSource Online (n.d.) *Parenting and Career Development*. Available at: *http://www.kidsource.com/ education/parenting.career.html* (accessed 20 July 2005).

Krashen, S. (1993) *The Power of Reading*. Englewood, CO: Libraries Unlimited.

Krueger, S. and Schmitt, R. (1999) *Reading Ability and the New Technologies – Developments in Germany.* Paper presented at the 65th IFLA Council and General Conference, Bangkok, Thailand, 20–28 August. See: *http://www.ifla.org/IV/ifla65/papers/115-145e.htm* (accessed 17 January 2007).

Kuhlthau, C.C. (1988) 'Meeting the information needs of children and young adults: basing library media programs on developmental states,' *Journal of Youth Services in Libraries*, 2 (1): 51–7.

Kuhlthau, C.C. and Todd, R. (2004) 'Student learning through Ohio School Libraries.' See: *http://www.oelma .org/StudentLearning/documents/OELMAReportofFindi ngs.pdf* (accessed 19 January 2007).

Lamb, S.M. (n.d.) *Neuro-Cognitive Structure in the Interplay of Language and Thought*. Available at: *http://www.ruf.rice.edu/~lamb/lt.htm* (accessed 10 August 2005).

Lance, K.C. and Russell, B. (2004) 'Scientifically based research on the impact of school librarians on academic achievement', *Knowledge Quest*, 32 (5): 13–17.

Leedy, P. and Ormrod, J. (2005) *Practical Research: Planning and Designing*, 8th edn. Upper Saddle River, NJ: Merrill Prentice Hall.

Lester, J. and Koehler, W.C. (2003) *Fundamentals of Information Studies: Understanding Information and Its Environment.* New York: Neal-Schuman.

Library and Information Services Council (1995) *Investing in Children: The Future of Library Services for Children and Young People*, Report of the Library and Information Services Council (England) Working Party on Library Services for Children and Young People, Department of National Heritage Library Information Series No. 22. London: HMSO.

Library of Congress (n.d.) 'Progressive era to new Era, 1900–1929: women's suffrage in the progressive era,' *The Learning Page.* Available at: *http://memory.loc.gov/learn/features/timeline/progress/suffrage/suffrage.html* (accessed 6 June 2006).

Lipsman, C.K. (1972) *The Disadvantaged and Library Effectiveness.* Chicago: American Library Association.

Long, H.G. (1969) *Public Library Service to Children: Foundation and Development.* Metuchen, NJ: Scarecrow Press.

Lorenzen, M. (2002) 'Deconstructing the philanthropic library: the sociological reasons behind Andrew Carnegie's millions to libraries.' See: *http://www.michaellorenzen.com/carnegie.html* (accessed 11 January 2007).

Lukenbill, W.B. (1977) 'Teaching helping relationship concepts in the reference process,' *Journal of Education for Librarianship*, 18 (2): 110–20.

Lundin, A. (1996) 'The pedagogical context of women in children's services and literature scholarship,' *Library Trends*, 44 (4): 840–50.

Lynch-Brown, C. and Tomlinson, C.M. (2005) *Essentials of Children's Literature*, 5th edn. New York: Pearson Education.

McCook, K. de la Peña (2004) *Introduction to Public Librarianship*. New York and London: Neal-Schuman.

Martin, L. (1963) *Students and the Pratt Library: Challenge and Opportunity*, Deiches Fund Studies of Public Library Service No. 1. Baltimore, MD: Enoch Pratt Free Library.

Matsui, T. (1997) 'The future of the Earth, which at length became round,' in O. Miyake (ed.), *Children's Rights in the Multimedia Age*. Lanham, MD: Scarecrow Press.

Mathews, V. (ed.) (1994) *Library Services for Children and Youth: Dollars and Sense*. Chicago: Neal-Schuman.

Matthews, V. (2004) 'Children couldn't wait then either, but sometimes they had to,' *American Libraries*, June/July: 76–80.

Mediavilla, C. (2001) 'Why library homework centers extend society's safety net,' *American Libraries*, 32 (12): 40–2.

Mississippi Library Commission (2004) *Resource Guide for Directors of Mississippi Public Library Systems*. Jackson, MS: Mississippi Library Commission.

National Center for Education Statistics (1988) *Survey Report: Services and Resources for Young Adults in Public Libraries*. Washington, DC: US Government Printing Office (ERIC Document Reproduction Service No. ED 301 199).

National Early Childhood Technical Assistance Center, Office of Special Education Programs, US Department of Education: *Part C of the Individuals with Disabilities Education Act (IDEA): Seventh in a Series of Updates on Selected Aspects of the Early Intervention Program for Infants and Toddlers with Disabilities*. See:

http://www.nectac.org/~pdfs/pubs/partcupdate2005.pdf (accessed 17 August 2006).

National Network for Child Care – see: *http://cyfernet.ces .ncsu.edu/cyfdb/browse_2pageAnncc.php?subcat=Child+ Development&search=NNCC&search_type=browse* (accessed 18 January 2007).

Neff, H. (1996) 'Strange faces in the mirror: the ethics of diversity in children's films', *The Lion and the Unicorn*, 20 (1): 50–65.

Norwell Regional Library System (n.d.) *120 Resources for Youth Services Librarians*. See: *http://www.norweld .lib.oh.us/ys/print_resources.htm* (accessed June 2006).

Notari-Syverson, A., O'Connor, R.E., and Vadasy, P.F. (1998) *Ladders to Literacy: A Preschool Activity Book*. Baltimore, MD: Paul H. Brookes Publishing.

Pawley, C. (2005) 'Gorman's gauntlet: gender and crying wolf,' *Journal of Education for Library and Information Science*, 46 (4): 304–11.

Peter D. Hart Research Associates (2001) *The Reading Habits of Adolescents Survey*. National Education Association.

Pfiel, A.B. (2005) *Going Places with Youth Outreach: Smart Marketing Strategies for Your Library*. Chicago: American Library Association.

Piaget, J. (1977) *The Development of Thought: Equilibration of Cognitive Structures*. New York: Viking Press.

Power, E. (1928) 'The organization and equipment of a children's room', in Committee on Library Work with Children of the American Library Association, *Children's Library Yearbook*. Chicago: American Library Association.

Power, E. (1930) *Library Service for Children*. Chicago: American Library Association.

Quek, S.K. and Higgins, S. (2003) 'The value of print literacy in the education of young children in Singapore', *International Journal of the Book*, 1 (3): 259–70.

Reichel, R. (1991) *Reference Services for Children and Young Adults*. Hamden, CT: Library Professional Publications.

Richey, C. (1993) *Programming for Children with Special Needs*, ALSC Program Support Publications. Chicago: American Library Association.

Rovenger, J. (1983) 'Nurturing intellectual curiosity: a practical look at reference services for children and young adults in public libraries,' *Reference Librarian*, 7 (8): 137–42.

Sannwald, W. (2000) 'Understanding organizational culture', *Library Administration and Management*, 14 (1): 8–14.

Sayers, F.C. (1965) *Summoned by Books: Essays and Speeches by Frances Clarke Sayers*. New York: Viking Press.

Sewell, M. (n.d.) *The Use of Qualitative Interviews in Evaluation*. See: *http://ag.arizona.edu/fcs/cyfernet/cyfar/Intervu5.htm* (accessed 9 March 2005).

Shenton, A.K. (2003) 'Youngsters' use of other people as an information seeking method,' *Journal of Librarianship and Information Science*, 35 (4): 219–33.

Shenton, A.K. and Dixon, P. (2003) 'Just what do they want? What do they need? A study of the informational needs of children,' *Children and Libraries*, 1 (2): 36–42.

Shenton, A.K. and Dixon, P. (2004a) 'The development of young people's information needs,' *Library and Information Research*, 28 (89), 25–34.

Shenton, A.K. and Dixon, P. (2004b) 'Young people's use of non-fiction books at home,' *Journal of Librarianship and Information Science,* 36 (2): 69–78.

Shiflett, L. (2000) 'Some speculation on the future of the book,' in B. Katz (ed.), *Readers, Reading and Librarians*. (Co-published simultaneously in *The Acquisitions Librarian*, 25: 35–49.)

Smith, K. (1996) 'Imagination and scholarship: the contributions of women to American children's and young adult literature and services,' *Library Trends*, 44 (4): 736–54.

Smith, L.H. (1939) 'The library's responsibility to the child,' in E.M. Danton (ed.), *The Library of Tomorrow: A Symposium*. Chicago: American Library Association.

Spelman, A. and Kelly, P. (2004) 'In visible light: illuminating partnerships across libraries to facilitate lifelong learning for young people,' *Aplis*, 17 (1).

Stan, S. (2003) 'A castle of books: visiting the International Youth Library,' *Children and Libraries*, 1 (3): 29–32.

Stricevic, I. (2005) *50th Anniversary of the Children's Section: History of the Section and Plans for the Future*. World Library and Information Congress, 71st IFLA General Conference and Council: 'Libraries – A Voyage of Discovery,' 14–18 August. Oslo: IFLA. Available online at *www.ifla.org* (accessed 3 August 2006).

Sullivan, M. (2005) *Fundamentals of Children's Services*, ALA Fundamental Series. Chicago: American Library Association.

Train, B. (2003) 'Reader development,' in J. Elkin, B. Train, and D. Denham, *Reading and Reader Development: The Pleasure of Reading*. London: Facet.

Train, B., Dalton, P., and Elkin, J. (2000) 'Embracing inclusion: the critical role of the library,' *Library Management*, 21 (9): 483–91.

Trelease, J. (2005) *The Read-Aloud Handbook*. East Rutherford, NJ: Penguin Books.

US Center for Education Statistics (n.d.) *Services and*

Resources for Children and Young Adults in Public Libraries. Washington, DC: US National Center for Education Statistics. Available online at: *http://nces.ed/gov/sruveys/frss/publications/95357/* (accessed 20 July 2006).

Usherwood, B. (2003) 'A framework with a fragile foundation: thoughts from a critical friend on Framework for the Future,' *Library Management*, 24 (6/7): 305–9.

Vandergrift, K. (1996) 'Female advocacy and harmonious voices: a history of public library services and publishing for children in the United States,' *Library Trends*, 44 (4): 683–718.

Vincent, J. (2005) *Public Libraries and Community Cohesion: A Paper for the South East Library Museum and Archives Council.* See: *http://www.mlasoutheast.org.uk/assets/documents/100005EAlibrariescommunitycohesion.pdf* (accessed 17 January 2007).

Vygotsky, L.S. (1987) *Mind in Society.* Cambridge, MA: Harvard University Press.

Walter, V.A. (2001) *Children and Libraries: Getting It Right.* Chicago and London: American Library Association.

Walter, V.A. (2003) 'Public library service to children and teens: a research agenda,' *Library Trends*, 51 (4): 571–89.

Walter, V.A. (2005) 'Teens are from Neptune, librarians are from Pluto: an analysis of online reference transactions,' *Library Trends*, 54 (2): 209–27.

Walter, V.A. (2006). 'Forward,' in E.T. Dresang, M. Gross, and L.E. Holt (eds), *Dynamic Youth Services through Outcome-Based Planning and Evaluation.* Chicago: American Library Association.

Weigand, W. (2006) 'Introduction: on the social nature of reading,' in *Genreflecting: A Guide to Popular Reading Interests.* Westport, CT: Libraries Unlimited.

Willett, H.G. (1995) *Public Library Youth Services: A*

Public Policy Approach. Norwood, NJ: Ablex.

Wyndham, L. (1989) *Writing for Children and Teenagers*. Cincinnati, OH: Writer's Digest Books.

Yohalem, N. and Pittman, K. (2003) *Public Libraries as Partners in Youth Development: Lessons and Voices from the Field*. Washington, DC: Forum for Youth Investment. See: *www.forumforyouthinvestment.org* (accessed 3 October 2006).

Young Adult Library Services Association (2003) *Young Adults Deserve the Best: Competencies for Librarians Serving Young Adults* – see: *http://www.ala.org/ ala/yalsa/professsionaldev/youngadultsdeserve.htm* (accessed 18 January 2007).

Young Sook Song (2006) *Family Reading in Children's Library Services of Korea*. World Library and Information Congress, 72nd IFLA General Conference and Council, 20–24 August 2006, Seoul, Korea. See: *http://www.ifla.org/IV/ifla72/papers/081-Song-en.pdf* (accessed 29 November 2006).

Youth Services Report (2002) *Youth Services in the New Hamilton Public Library System*. See: *http://www .myhamilton.ca/NR/rdonlyres/4E5AE266-BE17-4E78-AC51-AE99BC1D0AB3/15951/youthserv* (accessed 23 August 2006).

Zweizig, D.L. (1993) 'The children's services story,' *Public Libraries*, January/February: 26–8.

Useful websites

American Library Association (ALA) – see: *www.ala.edu*

Association for Library Services to Children (ALSC) – see: *http://www.ala.org/ala/alsc/alsc.htm*

Bulletin of the Centre for Children's Books – see: *http://bccb.lis.uiuc.edu/*

Chartered Institute of Library and Information Professionals (CILIP) – see: *http://www.cilip.org.uk/default.cilip*

Children's Book Council of Australia – see: *http://www.cbc.org.au/*

Georgia Public Library Services – see: *http://www.georgialibraries.org/lib/child.html*

International Board on Books for Young People – see: *http://www.ibby.org/*

International Children's Digital Library – see: *http://www.icdlbooks.org/*

International Federation of Library Associations (IFLA) – see: *http://www.ifla.org*

International Youth Library – see: *http://www.ijb.de/entry2.html*

Internet Public Library Youth Division – see: *http://www.dlib.org/dlib/january00/01featured-collection.html*

Library of Congress National Library Service for the Blind and Physically Handicapped – see: *http://www.loc.gov/nls/*

Live Homework Help – see: *http://www.tutor.com/ravingfans/rf_lhwh_lib.htm#arizona*

Mildred L. Batcheldor Award – see: *http://www.ala.org/ala/alsc/awardsscholarships/literaryawds/batchelderawar d/batchelderaward.htm*

National Dissemination Center for Children with Disabilities (NICHCY) – see: *http://www.nichcy.org/index.html*

Piaget, Jean – see: *http://www.ship.edu/~cgboeree/piaget.html*

Search Institute – see: *http://www.search-institute.org/*

Social Responsibilities Round Table (SRRT) – see: *http://libr.org/srrt/aboutus.html*

UNESCO Bangkok – see: *http://www.unescobkk.org/index.php?id=2179/news.htm*

Unicef – see: *http://www.unicef.org/protection/index_bigpicture.html*

VOYA (*The Voice of Youth Advocates*) – see: *http://www.voya.com/aboutus/index.shtml*

Vygotsky, Lev – see: *http://en.wikipedia.org/wiki/Lev_Vygotsky*

Young Adult Library Services Association – see: *http://www.ala.org/ala/yalsa/yalsa.htm*

Author index

Subject index

ABCs, 20
access point, 11
adolescence, 8, 27, 37, 54, 60, 67, 88, 108
adolescent psychology, 14
advocacy, 31
Aesop's Fables, 19
aesthetic appreciation, x
affective domain, 17
affective learning process, 28
ALA's Social Responsibilities Round Table, 9, 10
American heritage, 7
American Library Association (ALA), 4, 113
American way of life, 3
Americans with Disabilities Act, 43
anthropomorphism, 23
Ask a Librarian, 54
assimilation, 3
Association for Library Services to Children (ALSC), 106, 111

benchmarked, 51
benefits of reading, xi
bestiaries, 20
blogs, 11, 77
book selection, 79, 91
booklists, 29, 54
books, 30, 66

Brothers Grimm, 9

Captioned Media Program (CMP), 44
careers, 8
Carnegie Libraries, 19
censorship, 108
chapbooks, 20
chat discourse environment, 52
child development, 14, 50
Child Labor Laws, 4
Child Study Association, 19
childhood, 22, 67
children with disabililties, 43
children's librarianship, 32, 42, 55
Children's Rights Convention, 25
Christianity, 19
citizen, 3
cognition, 11
cognitive models, 14
collection, x, 16, 29, 38, 42
collection development policy, 42
collection provision, 8, 109
Columbia Library School, 9
commitment, xi
communication dimension, 32
communities of practice, 31
community, xi, 25, 41, 102, 122

Printed in the United Kingdom
by Lightning Source UK Ltd.
123084UK00001B/186/A